In MidLife

A Jungian Perspective

by

Murray Stein

Spring Publications, Inc.
Dallas, Texas

Seminar Series 15

Third Printing 1986

Published by Spring Publications, Inc.; P.O. Box 222069;
Dallas, Texas 75222. Printed in the United States of America

International distributors:
Spring; Postfach; 8800 Thalwil; Switzerland.
Japan Spring Sha, Inc.; 1–2–4, Nishisakaidani-Cho;
    Ohharano, Nishikyo-Ku; Kyoto, 610–11, Japan.
Element Books Ltd; Longmead Shaftesbury;
    Dorset SP7 8PL; England.

Cover design by Mary Vernon

Library of Congress Cataloging in Publication Data

Stein, Murray, 1943–
    In midlife : a Jungian perspective.

    (Seminar series ; 15)
    Bibliography: p.
    1. Middle age—Psychological aspects.   2. Identity
(Psychology)   3. Jung, C. G. (Carl Gustav),
1875–1961.   I. Title.   II. Series: Seminar series
(Spring Publications) ; 15.
BF724.6.S73   1983   158'.1'0880564   83-7482
ISBN 0-88214-115-5

For Jan, my companionable wife

Acknowledgments

There are many people whom I would like to acknowledge for their help and encouragement in bringing this work to its present form. Most of them, I'm sure, had no idea they were helping me, any more than I knew it, but isn't that the way of Hermes? Here is but a partial list of the friends, students, teachers, colleagues, and others who deserve mentioning: John Beebe, Sue Crommlin, Sharron Dorr, Paul Friedrick, Ruth Fry, Gene Gendlin, James Hillman, Pat Heugel, Russ Lockhart, Rafael Lopez-Pedraza, Boris Matthews, Louise Mahdi, Barbara McClintock, John Nicholas, June Nelson, Lee Roloff, Roland Rude, John Raphael Staude, Carolyn Stevens. I thank, too, the many people, whose names I do not know, who listened to these lectures and responded so warmly and enthusiastically to them. Above all, I thank the many analysands who have shown me the rich detail of the soul's journey at midlife, who must go unnamed but not unremembered by the author of these pages.

The figure behind the scenes is my wife, Jan Stein, a Gemini, from whom I have learned more about the world of Hermes than is told in all the books in Alexandria.

Contents

Introduction

The original title of this work, first presented as an eight-week seminar in the spring of 1980 at the C. G. Jung Center of Chicago, was ''The World of Hermes and the Experience of Liminality: Reflections on the Midlife Transition.'' It is a title too awkward for publication, but it does reflect quite truly the themes I am weaving together in this book.

This work is centrally about midlife and about what is today called ''the midlife transition'' or, more dramatically, ''the midlife crisis.'' So pervasive has the general awareness of this phenomenon become that as we approach this time of life we almost automatically begin to brace for a psychological emergency. Everyone seems to expect this illness at midlife, and if you don't think it's happening to you, at least you're quick to diagnose the disease in others. We see middle-aged friends and colleagues behaving in surprising ways; we feel something stirring deeply within ourselves as we approach this period in our own lives; and we want to know, quite understandably, what's going on and what to expect.

The midlife crisis typically brings about the astonishing recognition of our own hidden-away madness. What comes over us unexpectedly, and 'inappropriately,' in our middle years is a psychological state of affairs that can steal our pride and self-assurance and throw us into doubts about our emotional balance and mental health. Midlife crisis turns persons inside out and tears up their crafted worlds. Mothers and housewives discover Pan in their gardens and workshops, or Dionysos in the classroom: figures who come at them with all the force of preposterous and prepossessing gods demanding submission. Professors spy irresistible nixies in their graduate seminars and thrill to newfound libido, to enchanting visions of soulful delight and communion, and before they know it they have abandoned the library and the laboratory to rediscover the road of passion and adventure. Bankers, ministers, stock market operators, matrons, mothers—who will be next to drop the plow and begin responding to this improbable dance of life?

What has happened? At midlife, when we discover that the emotional turmoil and confusion, and the nightmares, of childhood and adolescence are not safely tucked away behind us, a myth is shattered. The psyche is still very much alive and active. The assumption that 'adulthood' is one long steady period of progressive growth (or decline) set upon an unshakable foundation and evenly monitored by an invisible parental eye must be a figment of childhood's imagination of adulthood. It is a view rooted in a parental imago, which is itself based on an archetypal pattern that reflects a child's need for and expectation of a solid bedrock of parenthood. If adults see children as polymorphously perverse, then the child in each of us wants to see adulthood as uniformly normal. But at midlife the psyche explodes, and the lava from this eruption forms and reforms the landscapes of our psychological lives.

The reason this happens at midlife calls for some attention. A shibboleth that circulates throughout the whole field of psychotherapy holds that the fault of adulthood's psychological turmoil should all be laid at the feet of defective childhood. If only childhood were good enough, adulthood would be tranquil. If this old psychoanalytic model of development were indeed true, nothing would remain to do therapeutically or developmentally after age five but to undo the wrongs that had been done earlier. Recent research has, if nothing else, exploded this fiction and has shown that adulthood is as 'developmental' as childhood or adolescence is. There is much still to be done, and many more developmental crises to endure, not only after the fifth year, but also after the thirty-fifth, after the fiftieth, even after the seventy-fifth. (If midlife is now opening to exploration in our modern psychology, the study of old age is still virgin territory.) We are beginning to realize that in *all* of life we are in psychological process and therefore subject to internal flux and change.

At midlife there is a crossing-over from one psychological identity to another. The self goes through a transformation. And it is the internal workings and the meaning of this crossing that I am exploring in the following pages and chapters. If I take as my primary data the events that are transpiring at midlife within the inner recesses of the psyche, I do this not in ignorance or disregard of the grave interpersonal and social ramifications of these momentous happenings within the hidden depths of the individual. But I consider midlife to be a time when persons are going through a fundamental shift in their alignment with life and with the world, and this shift has psychological and religious meaning beyond the interpersonal and social dimensions. Midlife is a crisis of the spirit. In this crisis, old selves are lost and new ones come into being.

For years I have wondered what it takes to become 'psychological.' What brings a person to attend the psyche, to respect its force, and to honor its gifts? What makes a person 'religious'? Whether attending to psyche, and being psychological, means at any given moment loving or hating the soul, at any rate it means keenly recognizing it and its workings. So what does it take to reach a point where, like Jung, you can say that the psyche is your worst curse and your greatest wealth? How does this attitude come about?

One way, I have concluded, is through psychological 'crisis.' When you are thrown into a psychological emergency, you cannot avoid seeing the soul at work. When things are going by plan, the soul sleeps, its realm as faded and vague as moon and stars in the brightness of the sun. Dreams and fantasies, the evidence of soul, exist, but they drift by obscurely and do not matter. Why attend to them? They only distract you. But in the dark night of psychological crisis, when the light of day is eclipsed, the figures of the psyche stand out and assume another magnitude. Dreams can strike like thunderbolts and leave you shaken to the core. It is in this night that Hermes comes forth and does his work. His myth speaks of the soul's awakening and emergence.

By the time that midlife comes, a person has usually settled into familiar psychological patterns and is ensconced in work and family. And then, suddenly, a crisis: you wake up one day and you are unexpectedly out of gas; the atmosphere of personal ownership stinks; the sweet milk of achievement is sour; the old patterns of coping and acting pinch your feet. The ability to prize your favorite objects—your 'works': children, possessions, power positions, accomplishments—has been stolen, and you are left wondering what happened last night? Where did it go?

Last night Hermes stole Apollo's cattle. (I am referring now to the myth of Hermes' birth, as told in the Homeric *Hymn to Hermes*.) The older brother god, Apollo, is surprised and angry. But he means to have his cattle back, and so, in anger and frustration, the search for the thief and for the lost treasure begins. This is the first act of the drama that unfolds at midlife: "What do you mean I've lost it? I'll get it back!"

But Apollo never does. The second act opens in Hermes' cave, where this tiny but already masterful thief lies innocently beside his mother. When you follow the tracks of the thief of your libido, moving backwards and down into the obscurity of the unconscious, you come upon the home of this cave-dweller in yourself. You have been ripped off by a sly and cunning newborn babe who has hooked your treasure and thrown you for a fall.

In this second act of the midlife drama, Hermes awakens the soul from its slumber and whisks away its ashes. In this period of psychological upheaval and turmoil, our bonds to parents and to society, to friends and to professional colleagues come frayed and undone. We don't care, we want freedom, we cry for depth and meaning. The psyche awakens.

Peering from his crib, Hermes feigns innocence. A thief, but an inventor too, Hermes is a force to be reckoned with. He is out to win a place for himself on Olympus, to seize fame and fortune for himself and for his mother, and he refuses anything less than full recognition of his birthright: he is a son of Zeus. He appears as a curse but also as a bringer of invention and delight. To everyone he is illegitimate, and to established order he is a threat. In midlife the soul, backed by this newly-hatched, renegade, inventive force, asserts itself and demands attention.

Hermes cannot be 'contained,' nor can the soul at midlife. Like Hermes, the soul slips out of confinement and demands to be seen, loved, honored. It must, too, be feared for its insistence and its determination to live and to be granted the glory it is owed. I offer no solutions to the midlife crisis in this book and few concrete suggestions for coping with the terrifying forces it sometimes triggers. I can only recommend a way of involvement, a Hermetic pathway into and through this travail of psyche. From myth we know that the conflict between Apollo, the elder, established brother, and Hermes, the upstart, illegitimate sibling, issues in an exchange of gifts between them. In the end, Apollo can have his cattle but now doesn't want them; instead, he receives an invention of Hermes', the lyre. I cannot specify what the gift of soul to you will be at midlife. I can only suggest that when it is presented it be received. This exchange constitutes the third act of the midlife drama.

For Apollo the gift was music, and this Hermetic plaything became for him his greatest and most singular attribute as a god. When the soul awakens at midlife and presents its gifts, life is permanently marked by the inclusion of them. Taken in, they become the hallmark of your life, the core of your uniqueness. Refused, they can haunt your days and may undermine all your toiling.

The god of journeyers, of boundaries and of boundary situations, who transfers messages and communications among the realms; the god of passages from one dimension of existence to another, from life to death and from death to life, who in alchemy becomes the master of transformations: Hermes is the one to whom I will look in the following odyssey for cues to advance our movement through the journey that opens up in midlife. In Hermes we may find companionship on the paths that appear from nowhere, and may lead anywhere, during this critical period of life. It may be then that we have little choice other than to let Hermes, guide of souls, be our guide also.

Chapter One

Hermes, Guide of Souls through Liminality

> He who moves about familiarly in this world-of-
> the-road has Hermes for his God.
>
> Kerényi

Since the Greek god Hermes is a leading figure in the psychological dramas to be explored throughout this book, it is fitting to begin by introducing him and by showing how he is linked to one of the central preoccupations in these reflections, the experience of psychological liminality. The presence, and the role, of the archetypal unconscious within transitional periods is a central theme of this book, and Hermes is a figure who represents this presence. As Dante had his Virgil, we will have Hermes as our guide into and out of the experience of the midlife transition and its Inferno of liminal existence.

In this chapter I address midlife itself only tangentially, the major objective here being to link Hermes and liminality and to set the stage for the later discussion of the archetypal aspects of the midlife transition and of the experience of liminality within it.

Hermes, the god of boundaries and of traffic over them, of pathways that wander over land and sea, of cultural spaces such as markets and bazaars where ambiguous exchanges take place, represents a type of consciousness that exists *essentially* within transitional time and space. Hermes is the god of transitions, and transitions always move through liminality. The "world of Hermes," as

Kerényi speaks of this archetype, is "existence in flux" (1976, p. 12), another definition for the experience of liminality. One of Hermes' epithets is *stropheus*, the "socket" on which a door turns: Hermes is *fixed* in liminality, and the world of Hermes is existence as liminality.

The term "liminality" is used throughout the text, so a few words need to be said about it before launching out into the body of the discussion.

The English "liminality" comes from the Latin *limen*, meaning 'doorway' or 'threshold.' Entering a room or leaving it, one crosses a *limen*, and while there, in this borderline space, one is in liminality, if only for a half second.

This Latin root has infiltrated psychology, where it is used to refer to a threshold between consciousness and the unconscious portions of the mind. So, the term "*sub*liminal" refers to psychological territory below the threshold of conscious awareness. This threshold is crossed and recrossed in going to sleep and awakening, and in the twilight state between the two, again, is liminality.

In our reflecting on the midlife transition and the experience of liminality within it, the world of Hermes therefore immediately suggests itself as a mythic, archetypal backdrop. But more than a backdrop of insight and perspective, the archetype that is represented by the Greek god Hermes reflects a sensed presence of the unconscious *whenever* life throws us into the state of liminality. Liminality triggers it into functioning. So whenever you are in liminality, Hermes is present. My explorations, therefore, are simply a matter of recording his presence and studying his ways to learn something about how to move within this ambiguous and often terrifying experience of being betwixt-and-between firm psychological structures and identifications.

In the state I am calling psychological liminality, a person's sense of identity is hung in suspension. You are no longer fixed to particular mental images and contents of yourself or others. The "I" is caught up in a field that it cannot control, whose patterns it does not recognize as "me." While the sense of "I-ness" and some of its continuities remain during liminality, the prevailing feeling is one of alienation, marginality, and drift. Critical questions arise as to who and what the "I" is, what it is capable of, where it comes from, where it is going. When the "I" is homeless, as it is in liminality, these Gnostic questions ring with considerable urgency, and they quite naturally open into religious areas of thought and feeling that are otherwise often closed.

In liminality the "I"'s standpoint is not fixed, and it occupies no clearly defined psychological location. It floats; it is not sharply delineated as "this" and "not that"; the boundaries between "I" and "not-I" blur and come much closer together than is true in the eras of fixed psychological identity. The ego is a has-been and a not-yet. Time warps: the ego forgets, the fixed edges of memory blur and fade, and the past juts forward in surprising and peculiar ways; the future has no particular image or contour. The "I" is not anchored to any particular inner images, ideas, or feelings. So, unattached, the "I" floats and drifts and wanders across many former boundaries and forbidden frontiers.

In liminality, too, there is an unusual degree of vulnerability to sudden emotional 'drafts' originating either within or without, to sudden moods and to highly charged images and thoughts, to sudden gains and losses of confidence. Inner ground shifts, and because the base is not firm a person can be easily influenced, pushed, and blown about. A sudden happening will make a more than normally deep impression, like an imprinting. More malleable in liminality than otherwise, a person may carry the effect of such imprintings through the rest of a lifetime.

This capsule description of psychological liminality prepares us to turn back to the earlier observation that in liminality Hermes is present. Since liminality is the realm of Hermes, his epiphany within it should be expected, but most likely, even so, it will come by surprise.

A story about Priam, king of the besieged city Troy, supplies an occasion for exploring the meaning of the idea that in liminality Hermes is present. In the Twenty-Fourth Book of the *Iliad* there is a scene in which Priam, the aged father of the recently slain Trojan hero, Hektor, is leaving the fortifications of Troy and going out of the city into the night. Slowly he makes his way through a dangerous no-man's land toward the camp of the Achaians, where he hopes to recover the body of his son.

This Book, the final one of the epic, opens with the conclusion of the athletic games held at the funeral of the Greek hero and friend of Achilleus, Patroklos. Achilleus has earlier revenged himself by killing Hektor, who slew Patroklos, and by dragging Hektor's corpse behind his chariot up and down the field of battle in front of the appalled onlookers on the walls of Troy. By this point, then, the Greeks have finished competing in their games; the funeral pyre has been ignited; the lamentations for Patroklos have subsided; ''and the people scattered to go away, each man to his fast-running ship, and the rest of them took thought of their dinner and of sweet sleep and its enjoyment; only Achilleus wept still as he remembered his beloved companion, nor did sleep who subdues all come over him'' (24: 1–5). And so he once more hitches up his horses and drags the corpse of Hektor around the smoldering funeral mound of his friend.

I take the opening of the Twenty-Fourth Book of the *Iliad* as a classic expression of a liminal period. It occurs during a war, and wartime is by itself a time of liminality for all but the most professional of soldiers. But this moment in the *Iliad* is particularly liminal, because it follows the climax of the story's action. It falls in the trough of the aftermath, in the period of mourning the losses brought about by the war's unpredictable fury. The battles of the epic are now over, as are the heroic games; the funeral has been thoroughly performed; and now begins the time of existing *without* the slain heroes, both Patroklos and Hektor. Achaians and Trojans alike have entered a period of intensified liminality. But the Trojans have still to bury their dead hero.

A loss of this magnitude—psychologically, it is a loss of the heroic defense—draws the psyche into liminality, which may be colored most heavily by feelings of grief for a lost past. Liminality is created whenever the ego is unable any longer to identify fully with a former self-image, which it had formed by selective attachments to specific internal imagos and embodied in certain roles accepted and performed. It had been embedded in a context created and supported by an archetypal pattern of self-organization, and now, since this matrix has dissolved or broken down, there is a sense of an amputated past and a vague future. Yet while this ego hangs there in suspension, still it remembers the ghost of a former self, whose home had been furnished with the presence of persons and objects now absent and had been placed in a psychological landscape now bare and uninhabitable without them. There is memory, too, perhaps, of status, of secured supremacy amidst a host of valiant defenders of the realm. But now all is different, and so it is to Priam, king of Troy and father of the slain hero Hektor, that I turn, for it is to Priam that Hermes will appear. Consider the reasons.

Homer's text relates that the gods become upset with Achilleus. Dragging the corpse of Hektor behind his chariot and his unquenchable thirst for revenge are offensive. The text says that the gods observing this scene "were filled with compassion and kept urging clear-sighted Argeiphontes to steal the body" (24: 23–24). *Naturally*, they would appeal to the archetypal thief, Hermes, to intervene and to spirit away the corpse of Hektor.

Lifting this text up for psychological insight, we can state that the unconscious in its archetypal depths—the realm of the gods—is burdened and offended by a situation that has developed in the conscious world, due in part to its own influence and interference. (The gods have been more than a little active on the battlefield of human affairs.) This condition of burden and upset provokes a response, a compensatory action, from the unconscious. Drawing this text closer for psychological inspection, we note that the compensatory action from the gods begins with a message, or rather with a series of messages: first the messenger Iris is sent to Thetis, mother of Achilleus; then Thetis is sent to her son; and finally Hermes is sent to Priam. To summarize much behind-the-scenes maneuvering, Zeus, through this flurry of message-sending, arranges an opportunity for Priam to retrieve Hektor's corpse, and Hermes plays a decisive role in this retrieval in several of his functions: as messenger, as guide, and as magician.

Hermes will appear to Priam, a figure who sums up the pathos of Troy as a whole. The sudden and surprising death of Hektor has thrown all of Troy into liminality. All its citizens recognize that dramatic change is imminent and unavoidable. The war they have fought bitterly for ten years looks like nothing more now than a prolonged defeat that is about to culminate in the savagery of taking spoils. And leading the procession of mourners and wailers along the ravaged walls of Troy is Priam, the aged king, a once proud father of a lately withered line of princes. It is to him in this doleful situation that Hermes will come, making one of his most renowned appearances in all of Greek story.

The stories of Hermes have him appearing in all the forms of liminality ranging from minor to major: within the micro- or mini-episodes of liminality—a sudden moment of darkness at noon—as well as in the macro-phases, or epochs, of liminality. Corresponding to the important distinction between micro-changes of attitude in individuals and macro-changes in their personality structures are these same types of liminality. Micro-changes occur in those small daily and hourly adjustments of psychic balance, brought about through relatively minor compensations from the unconscious, which keep us adapted and flexible and progressing through life, our defenses serviced and polished and at the ready. Related to these are moments, perhaps only flashes, of liminality. Macro-change, on the other hand, occurs throughout a much longer period of time, often extending over years, during which major attitudinal and typological shifts take place, basic psychological structures undergo dissolution, and archetypal patterns of self-organization become so deeply modified or re-formed as to constitute a definite transformation of the personality. Here much of the whole period is colored by the experience of psychological liminality.

The images of a city falling to its enemies and of an aged king being brought to the grave without an heir to replace and renew him symbolize the onset of an epoch of macro-change. And this change, whose alchemical parallel is the death and dissolution of the old king, takes place within an era of liminality. So it is at the beginning of this critical phase of transformation that we see King Priam: Troy is about to fall; its most vigorous defender, Hektor, is dead; and the inhabitants are afraid of the uncertain future. And it is a time for the dead to be honored, mourned, and decently buried.

It is to provide an honorable burial for Hektor's corpse, thereby putting his soul to rest, that the gods intervene. Hermes is chosen. Since one of Hermes' functions is to guide souls to the underworld, it is fitting that he should be the one to act for the gods in this situation. The gods do not, it should be noted, wish to revive Hektor or restore him to the living, so their intervention does not represent a compensatory wish-fulfillment. Hermes is not sent to help the grief-stricken Priam avoid the liminality that comes with collapse but rather to move him into it further and more cleanly. The unconscious does indeed aid the ego in coming to terms with deep-going, transformative change, but teleologically, and Hermes represents that helping factor: he guides the groping ego on the path to deeper liminality. Ultimately, this assistance will make it possible to accept mortality and separation from earlier heroic identifications and defenses and will prepare the ego for the next phase of individuation.

Hermes' role as guide of souls will be detailed throughout these chapters, but his role as messenger presents itself first for reflective consideration. In the *Iliad*, this messenger role is shared with Iris, a swift-footed, rainbow goddess. For the purposes of psychological reflection on the midlife transition and on the world of Hermes and liminality, we will consider her and Hermes to be expressions of the same unconscious psychological factor. What needs to be identified and discussed, then, is the message-sending function of the unconscious in this period of transition at midlife and its liminality. In liminality Hermes is present, first as a messenger from the archetypal unconscious.

When Iris comes with a message to the house of Priam, we see the grieving king for the first time in this Book:

> [Zeus] spoke, and storm-footed Iris swept away with the message
> and came to the house of Priam. There she found outcry and
>   mourning.
> The sons sitting around their father inside the courtyard
> made their clothes sodden with their tears, and among them
>   the old man
> sat veiled, beaten into his mantle. Dung lay thick
> on the head and neck of the aged man, for he had been rolling
> in it, he had gathered and smeared it on with his hands. And
>   his daughters
> all up and down the house and the wives of his sons were
>   mourning
> as they remembered all those men in their numbers and valour
> who lay dead, their lives perished at the hands of the Argives.
> The messenger of Zeus stood beside Priam and spoke to him

in a small voice, and yet the shivers took hold of his body:
"Take heart, Priam, son of Dardanos, do not be frightened.
I come to you not eyeing you with evil intention
but with the purpose of good toward you. I am a messenger
of Zeus, who far away cares much for you and is pitiful.
The Olympian orders you to ransom Hektor the brilliant,
to bring gifts to Achilleus which may soften his anger:
alone, let no other man of the Trojans go with you, but only
let one elder herald attend you, one who can manage
the mules and the easily running wagon, so he can carry
the dead man, whom great Achilleus slew, back to the city.
Let death not be a thought in your heart, you need have no fear,
such an escort shall go with you to guide you, Argeiphontes
who will lead you till he brings you to Achilleus. And after
he has brought you inside the shelter of Achilleus, neither
will the man himself kill you but will hold back all the others;
for he is no witless man nor unwatchful, nor is he wicked
but will in all kindness spare one who comes to him as a
    suppliant."
So Iris the swift-footed spoke and went away from him.

(24: 158–88)

Leaving aside the details of this message's content—clearly its overall intent is to encourage Priam—what are its implications for our theme, the psychological experience of transition at midlife? This is a message from the archetypal layers of the unconscious, coming at a point that can be identified as the critical beginning of a prolonged period of intense liminality. An analogous intervention in contemporary life is the event of an archetypal dream during the opening segment of an extended period of psychological destructuring, a time characterized chiefly by a sense of loss, by grief, by mourning.

The text is unambiguous about the reason the message comes at this particular moment: the gods are upset. Archetypal figures of the unconscious are disturbed by the situation developing in consciousness, and so they set into motion a compensating chain of events. These are designed to facilitate the grieving process, to enable the ego to get over loss by putting the ghost of the dead past to rest. If we understand the meaning of the message prospectively, it is the harbinger of a process that will open the way forward into a realm where Hermes can act as guide. This message is the first step in an unfolding sequence that will lead to the act of burial.

Assuming that Hermes will be present and will appear when you enter the realm of liminality, the question arises as to *how* he appears. How does Hermes come to you in liminality? The arrival of the messenger presents Priam with an experience of the uncanny: "shivers took hold of his body." Otto suggests that this is the key: "Always it is uncanny guidance that constitutes the essence of [Hermes'] activity" (p. 112). So how does uncanny guidance come from the unconscious when you enter the realm of intense liminality?

The text yields some hints for reflecting on this question. As Priam receives the message from Iris and sets out to act on it, the Homeric poet describes two levels of activity taking place simultaneously: one occurs at the level of human action, the other at the level of divine (archetypal) action:

> Now in urgent haste the old man mounted into his chariot
> and drove out through the forecourt and the thundering close.
>> Before him
> the mules hauled the wagon on its four wheels, Idaios
> the sober-minded driving them, and behind him the horses
> came on as the old man laid the lash upon them and urged them
> rapidly through the town, and all his kinsmen were following
> much lamenting, as if he went to his death. When the two men
> had gone down through the city, and out, and come to the flat
>> land,

the rest of them turned back to go to Ilion, the sons
and the sons-in-law. And Zeus of the wide brows failed not to
    notice
the two as they showed in the plain. He saw the old man and
    took pity
upon him, and spoke directly to his beloved son, Hermes:
"Hermes, for to you beyond all other gods it is dearest
to be man's companion, and you listen to whom you will, go now
on your way, and so guide Priam inside the hollow ships
of the Achaians, that no man shall see him, none be aware of him
of the other Danaans, till he has come to the son of Peleus."
    He spoke, nor disobeyed him the courier, Argeiphontes.
Immediately he bound upon his feet the fair sandals
golden and immortal, that carried him over the water
as over the dry land of the main abreast of the wind's blast.
He caught up the staff, with which he mazes the eyes of those
    mortals
whose eyes he would maze, or wakes again the sleepers. Holding
this in his hands, strong Argeiphontes winged his way onward
until he came suddenly to Troy and the Hellespont, and there
walked on, and there took the likeness of a young man, a noble,
with beard new grown, which is the most graceful time of young
    manhood.

                                                    (24: 322–48)

So a convergence between these two lines of action, the one originating on the human level, the other on the divine level, is in preparation, and this is how it looks to the human actor, King Priam:

    Now when the two had driven past the great tomb of Ilos
    they stayed their mules and horses to water them in the river,
    for by this time darkness had descended on the land; and the
        herald
    made out Hermes, who was coming toward them at a short
        distance.

He lifted his voice and spoke aloud to Priam: "Take thought,
son of Dardanos. Here is work for a mind that is careful.
I see a man; I think he will presently tear us to pieces.
Come then, let us run away with our horses, or if not, then
clasp his knees and entreat him to have mercy upon us."
  So he spoke, and the old man's mind was confused, he was
      badly
frightened, and the hairs stood up all over his gnarled body
and he stood staring. . . .

(24: 349–60)

As these two lines of action converge, Priam again experiences
the "uncanny." The figure he meets—"a young man, a noble, /
with beard new grown, which is the most graceful time of young
manhood" (24: 347–48)—is symbolic; he mediates an archetypal
background, and this is what lends this moment its uncanniness.
Something more than what the surface shows is stirring the psyche.
This is how Hermes appears: in an accidental meeting, as a figure
whose presence evokes an uncanny reaction, as though that figure
symbolized a far larger presence. Here two vectors meet, the one
representing the ego's intentionality, the other representing a
source of intention in the archetypal realm. And they converge in a
moment of synchronicity. This moment has the quality of unexpected luck, of *fortuna*. In a passage about Hermes, Otto writes:

> From him [i.e., Hermes] comes gain, cleverly calculated or wholly
> unexpected, but mostly the latter. That is his true characterization. If
> a man finds valuables on the road, if a man has a sudden stroke of
> luck, he thanks Hermes. . . . the favorable moment and its profitable
> exploitation are so much in the foreground that even thieves could
> regard themselves as his special protégés. (P. 108)

Hermes' presence is sudden gain, a stroke of luck, but the accent is
also strongly on the element of fear and the feeling of the uncanny.

With considerable justice, it can be said that the Greeks named the experience of synchronicity "Hermes." Hermes personifies the synchronistic moment. But it must be added that when he appears his epiphany takes place classically in the shadows or in the night, in liminal space and time. Or, the reverse occurs, and his presence brings about these shadows and this sense of time-out-of-time. He comes as a mild but uncanny shadow presence:

> . . . the kindly god himself coming closer
> took the old man's hand, and spoke to him and asked him a
>   question [*sic*]
> "Where, my father, are you thus guiding your mules and horses
> through the immortal night while other mortals are sleeping?
> Have you no fear of the Achaians whose wind is fury,
> who hate you, who are your enemies, and are near? For if one
> of these were to see you, how you are conveying so many
> treasures through the swift black night, what then could you think
>   of?
> You are not young yourself, and he who attends you is aged
> for beating off any man who might pick a quarrel with you.
> But I will do you no harm myself, I will even keep off
> another who would. You seem to me like a beloved father."
>   In answer to him again spoke aged Priam the godlike:
> "Yes, in truth, dear child, all this is much as you tell me;
> yet still there is some god who has held his hand above me;
> who sent such a wayfarer as you to meet me, an omen
> of good, for such you are by your form, your admired beauty
> and the wisdom in your mind. Your parents are fortunate in
>   you."

$$(24: 360-77)$$

Hermes' association with nighttime adds a further dimension to his identity as "Edgeman." In one of the most famous passages on Hermes ever penned by a classical scholar, Walter Otto offers a

vivid description, in his pages on ''Hermes and the night,'' of some
of the subtleties of liminality:

> . . . the marvellous and mysterious which is peculiar to night may also
> appear by day as a sudden darkening or an enigmatic smile. This
> mystery of night seen by day, this magic darkness in the bright
> sunlight, is the realm of Hermes, whom, in later ages, magic with
> good reason revered as its master. In popular feeling this makes itself
> felt in the remarkable silence that may intervene in the midst of the
> liveliest conversations; it was said, at such times, that Hermes had
> entered the room. . . . The strange moment might signify bad luck or
> a friendly offer, some wonderful and happy coincidence. (Pp. 117–18)

Otto's masterful description of night-consciousness describes
Hermes-consciousness as well, a consciousness at home in this
liminal world of ambiguity and unclear borders, nighttime:

> A man who is awake in the open field at night or who wanders over
> silent paths experiences the world differently than by day. Nighness
> vanishes, and with it distance; everything is equally far and near, close
> by us and yet mysteriously remote. Space loses its measures. There
> are whispers and sounds, and we do not know where or what they are.
> Our feelings too are peculiarly ambiguous. There is a strangeness
> about what is intimate and dear, and a seductive charm about the
> frightening. There is no longer a distinction between the lifeless and
> the living, everything is animate and soulless, vigilant and asleep at
> once. What the day brings and makes recognizable gradually, emerges
> out of the dark with no intermediary stages. The encounter suddenly
> confronts us, as if by a miracle: What is the thing we suddenly
> see—an enchanted bride, a monster, or merely a log? Everything
> teases the traveler, puts on a familiar face and the next moment is ut-
> terly strange, suddenly terrifies with awful gestures and immediately
> resumes a familiar and harmless posture.
> Danger lurks everywhere. Out of the dark jaws of the night which
> gape beside the traveller, any moment a robber may emerge without

warning, or some eerie terror, or the uneasy ghost of a dead man—who knows what may once have happened at that very spot? Perhaps mischievous apparitions of the fog seek to entice him from the right path into the desert where horror dwells, where wanton witches dance their rounds which no man ever leaves alive. Who can protect him, guide him aright, give him good counsel? The Spirit of the Night itself, the genius of its kindliness, its enchantment, its resourcefulness, and its profound wisdom. She is indeed the mother of all mystery. The weary she wraps in slumber, delivers from care, and she causes dreams to play about their souls. Her protection is enjoyed by the unhappy and persecuted as well as by the cunning, whom her ambivalent shadows offer a thousand devices and contrivances. With her veil she also shields lovers, and her darkness keeps ward over all caresses, all charms hidden and revealed. Music is the true language of her mystery—the enchanting voice which sounds for eyes that are closed and in which heaven and earth, the near and the far, man and nature, present and past, appear to make themselves understood.

But the darkness of night which so sweetly invites to slumber also bestows new vigilance and illumination upon the spirit. It makes it more perceptive, more acute, more enterprising. Knowledge flares up, or descends like a shooting star—rare, precious, even magical knowledge.

And so night, which can terrify the solitary man and lead him astray, can also be his friend, his helper, his counsellor. (Pp. 118–20)

Nighttime, then, this rich and evocative symbol of liminality, is the proper element of Hermes, the context in which he appears, and the context he evokes whenever he appears.

In concluding this chapter, I want to recapitulate some of the questions posed in the preceding pages and to summarize some of the reflections put forward so far. If we say that Hermes is present when we are in liminality, what does this mean in contemporary psychological terms and experience? What do we look for in searching out his presence? How do we recognize Hermes within the experience of liminality? Who, or what, is Hermes?

Liminality, Hermes' home, occurs: when the ego is separated from a fixed sense of who it is and has been, of where it comes from and its history, of where it is going and its future; when the ego floats through ambiguous spaces in a sense of unbounded time, through a territory of unclear boundaries and uncertain edges; when it is disidentified from the inner images that have formerly sustained it and given it a sense of purpose. Then, the unconscious is disturbed in its archetypal layers, and the Self is constellated to send messages: big dreams, vivid and powerful intuitions, fantasies, and synchronistic and symbolic events. The function of these messages is to lead the ego forward, and this guidance helps it to do what it has to do, whether this is to enter liminality further or, later, to emerge out of it. (Hermes, as will be detailed later, leads the soul both into and out of that most radical of symbols of liminality in Greek myth, the underworld.) Liminality, precisely, is the psychological territory in which the Hermetic message and Hermes' guidance befall the voyager. So, to the question of "who," or "what," appears to us as Hermes when we are in liminality, I would respond: it is the archetypal Self in the form of messenger and guide.

Chapter Two

Burying the Dead

The Entry into the Midlife Transition

> Midway this way of life we're bound upon,
> I woke to find myself in a dark wood,
> Where the right road was wholly lost and gone.
> Dante

Midlife is a time when persons often come unhinged and lose their footing in a secure social and psychological world. They make radical changes of many kinds, uproot themselves and move, and wander the earth restlessly looking for something, but what? The lines from Dante's *Inferno* quoted above offer an image for the state of mind that comes over persons at midlife as they enter a terrain that seems dark, unmarked, and lonely. For many it is truly a long dark night of the soul, a descent into regions of feeling and of experiencing that comes quite unexpected and certainly unsolicited. Midlife befalls us; we don't ask for it.

The awareness that midlife is often a troubled period in a person's life is not particularly new or sequestered from the public domain, and yet the difficulties of this period and the types of experience that occur during it often surprise us by their intensity and nature. We didn't think it would happen to *us*! Somehow we don't expect life to be this way in our mid-to-late thirties and early forties. And one of the most intense and surprising aspects of it is what I am calling the experience of liminality. This experience is a basic component of all transitional periods in life, and its powerful appearance at midlife marks this period as strongly transitional.

In the preceding chapter, I observed some of the many ways in which the world of Hermes forms the archetypal background of the common human experience of liminality. Himself the center of this world, Hermes represents a type of consciousness that is completely at home in liminal space and time. I reflected, too, on how the unconscious becomes palpable during liminality as uncanny symbolic events or figures, as synchronicity, as dreams and intuitive knowledge, and on how it leads a person unerringly to the first major task to be confronted in the prolonged transitional period ahead: the burial of a lost and grieved past image of identity and security.

In this chapter the core theme is *separation*, the first phase in the long process of psychological change that occurs at midlife. I want to extend the implications of this phase as far as possible beyond the commonplace observation that middle-aged men and women often become anxious and distressed because they see youthfulness slipping away from them. This phase of the midlife transition has dimensions of depth and complexity far beyond simply the forfeiture of youth's beauties, attractive and important as these are. To misread the midlife period as a crisis in cosmetics betrays a transparent defense against its far more gripping anxieties.

As the midlife transition begins, whether it begins gradually or abruptly, persons generally feel gripped by a sense of loss and all of its emotional attendants: moody and nostalgic periods of grieving for some vaguely felt absence, a keen and growing sense of life's limits, attacks of panic about one's own death, and exercises in rationalization and denial. Sometimes the reason for this sense of loss is obvious: the death of children or parents, a divorce, an obliterated career. But quite often the immediate cause of this opening phase of the transition, with the attendant emotional phenomena, is not at all plain. And even when the cause does seem blatant, a person will often go on searching anxiously and vainly, looking for another deeper cause of this distress, because acknowledging the obvious one does not pluck the thorn of pain. This thorn may be extremely hard to find because of its deep unconsciousness, and a person cannot seem to get to it and resolve the anxiety it is creating.

The fundamental cause of this distress is separation, and the anxiety about it is a type of separation anxiety. But separation from what? If it can't be pinned to nests emptying of children, or to careers collapsing, or to parents dying, or to mates divorcing, then separation from what? A person needs to find this corpse before it can be buried. The exact and deepest cause of the sense of loss must therefore be discovered before the healing words of benediction can be spoken over it.

The need to find this corpse is perhaps what has motivated, at least in part, the production of the currently still accumulating body of literature on the midlife transition. In the last two decades especially, midlife and its crises have drawn a lot of attention. Sociologists and psychologists have begun studying this period in detail, and writers of popular books and articles following in their wake have exercised little restraint in commercializing it. The topic has a market because there is a need to know what happens and what goes wrong during this period of psychological upheaval and turmoil.

Typically, the midlife transition lasts several years and occurs somewhere between the ages of thirty-five and fifty, usually falling around the age of forty (Levinson). Most students of it agree on certain characteristic features: there are often persistent moods of lassitude and depression, or feelings of disillusionment and disappointment either in life generally or in specific persons who have been formerly idealized; youth's dreams of happiness and fulfillment melt away or are rudely shattered; death anxiety steals in, and a sense that time will run out before one can get down to 'really liv- ing' is frequently reported; physically a person is beginning to show some signs of aging, and so an earlier self-image starts cracking and altering. It may be a time, too, when parents are either dying or becoming dependent on their children, thus reversing earlier roles and disabusing these children of illusions about immortality. And a person's own children may be achieving some measure of separation and independence, and this threatens change and the loss of love and of comfortable illusions of omnipotence.

Beneath the weltering of these moods and often vague threats of holes and gaps opening up under one's feet, a lot of deep restructur- ing is going on in the intrapsychic matrix of the personality, restruc- turing indicated primarily by dreams but also by such psychological phenomena as visions and persistent fantasies and intuitions—all of these being dark and often quite opaque messages from the un- conscious. Jung himself experienced the midlife transition as an in- tense emotional turning point in his life, calling it a "confrontation with the unconscious" (1961, pp. 170–99), and he conceptualized its stages and levels in one of his key psychological works, the much edited and rewritten *Two Essays in Analytical Psychology*. What he describes there is the breakdown of the *persona*, a psychological structure that is the approximate equivalent of what Erik Erikson calls the psychosocial *identity*, accompanied by the release of two hitherto repressed and otherwise unconscious elements of the per- sonality: the rejected and inferior person one has always fought becoming (the *shadow*), and behind that the contrasexual "other," whose power one has always, for good reason, denied and evaded (the *animus* for a woman, the *anima* for a man).

The threat created by this degree of intense internal restructur- ing, Jung observed, can produce a defensive "reconstitution of the persona," a retrenchment and retreat into former patterns of iden- tity and their defenses. On the other hand, this era of change can create movement into depth, into unknown and threatening psychological territory. A prolonged psychological journey of this kind, Jung felt, could lead a person to discover the core of his being, the Self. This discovery of the Self, and the gradual stabilization of its felt presence and guidance within conscious life, would become the foundation for a new experience of identity and integrity, based on an internal center, the Self, rather than rooted in externals, the cues and reinforcements from parental figures and other 'models,' from cultural influences and expectations, and from collective pressures. What one can gain from going all the way *through* the midlife transition, then, is the sense of an internal non-egoistic Self and the feeling of integrity and wholeness that results from living in conscious contact with it. Through his own midlife experience, Jung discovered himself and his vocation as a healer and as an originative psychological thinker; he found his "destiny" (cf. Jung 1961, p. 199; Ellenberger, pp. 698–703).

The midlife transition and crisis, then, involve making this crucial shift from a persona-orientation to a Self-orientation. This shift is critical for the individuation process as a whole, because it is the change by which a person sheds layers of familial and cultural influence and attains to some degree of uniqueness in his appropriation of internal and external facts and influences. And like other rites of passage, this transition can be divided into three stages: separation, liminality, and reintegration.

So far I have been reflecting only on the first of these, separation. From an intrapsychic point of view, then, what needs to be separated from in the first phase of the midlife transition is an earlier identity, the *persona*. The ego needs to let go of this attachment before it can float through the necessary period of liminality that is preliminary to a deeper discovery of the Self. To do this thoroughly and decisively, the person needs to "find the corpse" and then to bury it: to identify the source of pain and then to put the past to rest by grieving, mourning, and burying it. But the nature of the loss needs to be understood and worked through before a person can go on.

To speak of *persona*, however, and of the need to separate from it as being the fundamental issues for this first phase of the transition keeps the discussion too general and abstract, so I will now try to specify more concretely what this means by turning to the *Iliad* again and to the dilemma of King Priam as he makes his way toward the Achaian camp to recover the corpse of his slain son Hektor. It is Hektor's defeat and death that have brought Priam to this sorry pass of panic, loss, and bereavement. Hektor is the corpse. So who is Hektor, and how can this loss help us to understand the essence of this stage of the midlife transition?

The psychological meaning of Hektor's death begins and ends with the fact that he is a hero, debatably the greatest hero of the *Iliad*. He towers above his peers, both friend and foe, and represents the bulwark in Troy's defense against the foreign invader, as through the years of battle he matches the Greeks stride for stride and blow for blow on the battlefield. Hektor sums up their shared ideal of manly prowess, and for this ideal he is himself forced to sacrifice fatherhood to his small son, Astyanax, and husbandhood to the beautiful and queenly Andromache. So while Hektor represents an ideal, he also represents a figure utterly driven and controlled by it. The inevitable tragedy of his inability to relinquish this ideal is foreseen by Hektor himself. In a passage that is to my mind the most poignant in the entire *Iliad*, Hektor expresses his awareness of the fatefulness of his absolute ego-identification with this archetypally-based *persona*.

> So the housekeeper spoke, and Hektor hastened from his home backward by the way he had come through the well-laid streets. So as he had come to the gates on his way through the great city,

the Skaian gates, whereby he would issue into the plain, there
at last his own generous wife came running to meet him,
Andromache, the daughter of high-hearted Eëtion;
Eëtion, who had dwelt underneath wooded Plakos,
in Thebe below Plakos, lord over the Kilikian people.
It was his daughter who was given to Hektor of the bronze helm.
She came to him there, and beside her went an attendant carrying
the boy in the fold of her bosom, a little child, only a baby,
Hektor's son, the admired, beautiful as a star shining,
whom Hektor called Skamandrios, but all of the others
Astyanax—lord of the city; since Hektor alone saved Ilion.
Hektor smiled in silence as he looked on his son, but she,
Andromache, stood close beside him, letting her tears fall,
and clung to his hand and called him by name and spoke to him:
        "Dearest,
your own great strength will be your death, and you have no pity
on your little son, nor on me, ill-starred, who soon must be your
        widow;
for presently the Achaians, gathering together,
will set upon you and kill you; and for me it would be far better
to sink into the earth when I have lost you, for there is no other
consolation for me after you have gone to your destiny—
only grief; since I have no father, no honoured mother.
It was brilliant Achilleus who slew my father, Eëtion,
when he stormed the strong-founded citadel of the Kilikians,
Thebe of the towering gates. He killed Eëtion
but did not strip his armour, for his heart respected the dead man,
but burned the body in all its elaborate war-gear
and piled a grave mound over it, and the nymphs of the
        mountains,
daughters of Zeus of the aegis, planted elm trees about it.
And they who were my seven brothers in the great house all went
upon a single day down into the house of the death god,
for swift-footed brilliant Achilleus slaughtered all of them

as they were tending their white sheep and their lumbering oxen;
and when he had led my mother, who was queen under wooded
	Plakos,
here, along with all his other possessions, Achilleus
released her again, accepting ransom beyond count, but Artemis
of the showering arrows struck her down in the halls of her
	father.
Hektor, thus you are father to me, and my honoured mother,
you are my brother, and you it is who are my young husband.
Please take pity upon me then, stay here on the rampart,
that you may not leave your child an orphan, your wife a
	widow,
but draw your people up by the fig tree, there where the city
is openest to attack, and where the wall may be mounted.
Three times their bravest came that way, and fought there to
	storm it
about the two Aiantes and renowned Idomeneus,
about the two Atreidai and the fighting son of Tydeus.
Either some man well skilled in prophetic arts had spoken,
or the very spirit within themselves had stirred them to the
	onslaught.''
	Then tall Hektor of the shining helm answered her: ''All
	these
things are in my mind also, lady; yet I would feel deep shame
before the Trojans, and the Trojan women with trailing
	garments,
if like a coward I were to shrink aside from the fighting;
and the spirit will not let me, since I have learned to be valiant
and to fight always among the foremost ranks of the Trojans,
winning for my own self great glory, and for my father.
For I know this thing well in my heart, and my mind knows it:
there will come a day when sacred Ilion shall perish,
and Priam, and the people of Priam of the strong ash spear.
But it is not so much the pain to come of the Trojans

that troubles me, not even of Priam the king nor Hekabe,
not the thought of my brothers who in their numbers and
    valour
shall drop in the dust under the hands of men who hate them,
as troubles me the thought of you, when some bronze-
    armoured
Achaian leads you off, taking away your day of liberty,
in tears; and in Argos you must work at the loom of another,
and carry water from the spring Messeis or Hypereia,
all unwilling, but strong will be the necessity upon you;
and some day seeing you shedding tears a man will say of you:
'This is the wife of Hektor, who was ever the bravest fighter
of the Trojans, breakers of horses, in the days when they
    fought about Ilion.'
So will one speak of you; and for you it will be yet a fresh
    grief,
to be widowed of such a man who could fight off the day of
    your slavery.
But may I be dead and the piled earth hide me under before I
hear you crying and know by this that they drag you captive."
  So speaking glorious Hektor held out his arms to his baby,
who shrank back to his fair-girdled nurse's bosom
screaming, and frightened at the aspect of his own father,
terrified as he saw the bronze and the crest with its horse-hair,
nodding dreadfully, as he thought, from the peak of the
    helmet.
Then his beloved father laughed out, and his honoured mother,
and at once glorious Hektor lifted from his head the helmet
and laid it in all its shining upon the ground. Then taking
up his dear son he tossed him about in his arms, and kissed
    him,
and lifted his voice in prayer to Zeus and the other immortals:
"Zeus, and you other immortals, grant that this boy, who is
    my son,

may be as I am, pre-eminent among the Trojans,
great in strength, as am I, and rule strongly over Ilion;
and some day let them say of him: 'He is better by far than his
    father,'
as he comes in from the fighting; and let him kill his enemy
and bring home the blooded spoils, and delight the heart of his
    mother.''
    So speaking he set his child again in the arms of his beloved
wife, who took him back again to her fragrant bosom
smiling in her tears; and her husband saw, and took pity upon
    her,
and stroked her with his hand, and called her by name and
    spoke to her:
''Poor Andromache! Why does your heart sorrow so much for
    me?
No man is going to hurl me to Hades, unless it is fated,
but as for fate, I think that no man yet has escaped it
once it has taken its first form, neither brave man nor coward.
Go therefore back to our house, and take up your own work,
the loom and the distaff, and see to it that your handmaidens
ply their work also; but the men must see to the fighting,
all men who are the people of Ilion, but I beyond others.''
    So glorious Hektor spoke and again took up the helmet
with its crest of horse-hair, while his beloved wife went
    homeward,
turning to look back on the way, letting the live tears fall.
                          (6: 390–496. Italics added.)

Hektor's resignation in the face of what he calls ''fate'' amounts
to recognition that he cannot develop past the *persona*. He is
trapped in a role and an identity that, no matter where it takes him,
must be followed.

So what is lost through the death of Hektor is the hero and the
heroic ideal. When the hero is slain, there is a crumbling of defen-

sive structures, and the energy that once poured through this pattern of behavior is blocked or scattered.

If we stay for a moment with the concept of psychic energy, *libido*, we recognize that the "hero" represents a specific configuration and movement of it: libido moving dynamically forward—into sometimes adaptive and often defensive directions—but essentially in an expansive motion outward and forward. Even in defense the hero is expansionistic and offensive: taking the initiative, catching the enemy by surprise, overwhelming him with superior force and aggressive strategy. The heroic pattern is the "progression of libido" (to use the technical Jungian terms) in a phallic, expansionistic modality, taking charge and winning glory.

This mode of functioning comes to serious crisis through the experience of a clearcut defeat, especially if the defeat is large enough and occurs at a critical moment in life, such as the midlife point. Then a 'crack' can open in the identity between the ego and this persona, between "who I now feel I am" and "who I have appeared to be in my own eyes and in the eyes of others in the past." The glimpse into this discrepancy can be terrifying. When that former identity and the dreams it was based upon get deflated and lost, there is a sudden realization of the ego's vulnerability and of the shadow personality, as well as of the limits on life's ascendance and on its expansive movements forward. When Hektor is killed, limitation is experienced as *absolute*, as a door firmly closed forever, and death and defeat are taken as the final words on life.

This moment of conscious realization is critical for the purpose of separating from a former persona identification. Without the full absorption of it, the ego's natural defenses will snap the persona back into place and do their best to restore identification with it, even though it may now appear a little false and worn but still, for all its cracks, intact and affording more security than being exposed without it. So in order for separation to occur fully, there must be a full stop here, as this new psychological situation is absorbed. And in this period libido is scattered and has no discernible direction. It isn't going anywhere, forward or backward. And this stop continues until the dead body of Hektor can be recovered and properly buried, i.e., until disidentification from the pattern he represents, the former dominant pattern of libido organization, has been completed. The element of finality must be digested and absorbed, and the attachment to that past structure must be put to rest.

A person may experience a critical defeat at midlife, of course, without its resulting in this 'full stop' of inventory-taking and conscious separation from an earlier persona identification. Terrified at the prospect of facing the future without a familiar persona-linked identity, this man or woman invents the illusion that nothing is actually different. So he (or she) will persevere in holding on to an earlier pattern even after it has long since outlived its usefulness and has effectively undergone demise.

Here the corpse does not get buried but is instead propped up. But this is no longer adaptive, and a certain psychological 'stench' can be detected in this person's increasingly rigid, outmoded, and anxious behavior. And then, before separation has been completed, liminality begins, and the ego, not yet freed from its identification with the former persona to 'float' through this ambiguous period, is wrenched from its moorings and, unable to bury the past, is convulsed by waves of remorseful nostalgia. Who has not known a man whose climb to the top was to everyone but himself decisively halted, yet who kept dressing up to go to work and forcing himself to believe this was only a pause in the ascent, as he continued pursuing the same goal, all the while being profoundly uncommitted to it, and struggling manfully against a compulsion to run off with his secretary or his neighbor's wife? Or a woman who refused to stop mothering or playing the ingenue? While vitality has clearly ceased filling the forms of the old patterns, now maladaptive, the ego refuses to face loss and bury the past and therefore cannot enter the state of 'floating' that would lead back and downward into the unformed and unknown depths of the psyche.

The problem of an unresolved and incomplete separation from the earlier persona identification is created by a person's natural and wholly understandable desire to deny what has happened and to refuse all terms in dealing with major loss and the changes it portends. This kind of defensive denial of changing conditions, outer and inner, can be overcome only by "finding the corpse" and facing death in a concrete and unforgettable, irrevocable way.

So how can the corpse be found and retrieved when there are so many hindrances and defenses in the way? In the episode from the *Iliad* that I have been taking as paradigmatic for this phase of the midlife transition, it is Hermes who leads Priam through the night stealthily past the lines of the Greeks into the heart of their camp, where Achilleus himself watches over Hektor's body. Hermes plays the key role in first leading Priam to the corpse and then helping him to retrieve it. This action of finding and retrieving the corpse means that the ego has discovered a way through the lines of defense into the seat of its own anxiety about loss, death, and finality. In Hermes, the unconscious shows a figure who is able to control the functioning of these defenses.

All of the archetypes control consciousness, each in its own way, and Hermes does so by the magic of his staff "with which he mazes the eyes of those mortals whose eyes he would maze, or wakes again the sleepers" (*Iliad* 24: 343–44). Hermes is a magician who is able to lull the defenses to sleep and also to alert them and wake them up to danger. And he works by stealth rather than by force. In the *Homeric Hymn to Hermes*, the newborn god is seen slipping through a keyhole—"And Hermes, the son of Zeus, slipped through the keyhole of the dwelling sideways, like autumnal breeze in outer form, or airy mist" (145–47)—and this quality of stealth, in combination with his hypnotic magical power over the defenses against consciousness, describes the way in which this archetype works to lead a person past defenses into the guarded places of the unconscious. Hermes is the guide of the soul to the underworld, and he leads Priam to the place of the corpse, where death will be faced and grief will meet its maker. This encounter with death also brings consciousness of a dead past that needs to be buried.

To illustrate these Hermes-effects of the unconscious, I will relate a dream of A., a woman in her mid-thirties. In the previous chapter I suggested that the presence of Hermes could be detected in dreams and synchronistic events. A.'s dream and the life context surrounding its occurrence, I submit, show how the unconscious itself subtly introduces the themes of separation, finality, and death at the precise moment when these psychological tasks confront this woman in the first phases of her midlife transition. All of this together—the dream and the events surrounding it—I am taking as a signal of Hermes' activity and guidance.

A. dreamed that she was at the home of her grandmother (who in fact had been dead for many years but was present in the dream). The occasion is a family reunion, and A. is with hundreds of people gathered together from everywhere. Suddenly A. misses her eight-year-old son and sets out to find him. As she makes her way through the crowd, she overhears a woman speaking to a child and realizes this is her grandmother's companion, but the child is not her son, and the companion is black (in reality she had been white). At this point A. receives a phone call from her sister-in-law, who tells her that her mother (i.e., the sister-in-law's mother) has just died. She goes on to say how grateful she is that she had been able to build a good relationship with her mother before this unexpected death occurred. After their conversation is over, a young woman, about seventeen years of age, comes up to A. and embraces her.

A. realizes with a start that this young woman has recently died, and she wonders how it can be possible that she is at the party. A. concludes her dream report with: "She embraces me; 'but,' I say to myself, 'she's dead!'"

Clearly the theme of this dream is death. Variations on this single theme run through it like a leitmotif through Wagnerian opera. To begin with, the dream is set in a kind of "land of the dead," the grandmother being dead and her house therefore representing a "house of the dead." The grandmother's companion, too, is dead, as A. learned a few days before she had this dream. And the companion's 'blackness' in the dream may be the sign of an archetypal association with death and with the land of the dead, following Hillman's suggestion on the interpretation of blackness in dreams in his book *The Dream and the Underworld* (pp. 144–46). Then there is the conversation about the death of the sister-in-law's mother and about her dealing with that loss. (A.'s mother, on the other hand, who is still alive, does not appear in the dream, and this absence may add confirmation that the dream's psychological location is in the land of the dead, the lost and forever gone past.) And then there is the detail of the lost child and the dreamer's worries about him, which was a recurrent dream theme for her and always implied the fear of loss and separation and ultimately of death.

Most important of all, though, is the final scene, the *lysis* of the dream and its punchline. The girl who comes up to the dreamer and embraces her is the figure of a person who had actually died in her youth of an overdose of drugs. So the point of the dream, or the point the dream brings A. to, is the realization that this young girl, a *puella* figure, is *dead*. In the moment of embrace, A. grasps the death of this figure, who is also a figure of death, in a shocking and unforgettable way. In the dream as a whole, and especially in this dramatic conclusion, I see the hand of Hermes at work, lending resourceful and surprising guidance into this land of the dead, where

A. must discover the corpse she needs to bury. The corpse turns out to be a *puella* figure, the young girl she once was but can be no longer. In Greek mythology, this figure—a girl taken by death and transported to the land of the dead in her youth—was named Persephone and was seen as the Queen of Hades.

This dream is one event in a convergence of events in A.'s life at this time; together they make up a kind of synchronistic cluster. At the time of the dream, A. was about to enter a second marriage. She had spent the previous two years coming to terms with her divorce from a man to whom she had been married for some ten years. When she married him in her early twenties, she had not yet separated psychologically from her own family. The circumstances of this marriage had been so abrasive and threatening to her that she had stayed more or less arrested in her development for most of the following ten years. Toward the end of that marriage, she had begun making up for lost time, shedding many layers of her former innocence and dependency, and gaining psychological stature in relation to powerful figures in her world, particularly toward a rather overbearing father. So by the time of this dream, A. was, for the first time in her life, approaching psychological readiness for marriage. But to create this new dominant pattern of libido organization and identity, the ''wife'' or *sponsa*, the ground has to be cleared through the death and burial of the former pattern, the *puella*. So the dream leads her to the corpse that she still needs to recognize as dead and needs to bury in order to move into the next stage of individuation.

Actual deep-going psychological separation from an earlier persona, and from the sense of identity that goes with it, seems to require both a conscious and an unconscious recognition of the change. When change is acknowledged only superficially, by consciousness alone, but is not also worked through and accepted at the level of the unconscious, corpses tend to end up getting hidden rather than buried. The former identifications simply get covered over and partially concealed from view, but they continue to influence consciousness and behavior in many subtle and indirect ways. This had happened to A. in her previous marriage: the *puella* had been abandoned officially at the surface when her father walked her down the aisle and gave her over to a husband, but this former identity had not actually been buried. So married life was full of depression and vague longing, nostalgia, and regret. Because the psyche as a whole had not recognized and accepted the change A. had made at one level, it would not commit itself to a new pattern. So now the dead *puella* still had to be embraced, mourned, and buried by A.'s whole being before she could actually pledge herself as ''wife'' (*sponsa* = 'wife,' from *spondeo* = 'to pledge oneself') and before this new pattern could come fully into its own.

In associating to the dream, A. recalled that she had been given the dead girl's diary to read a few days before the dream occurred and that she had been fascinated by its contents. The dream itself came, moreover, while she was visiting her parents for the holidays. This visit, A. reported, had been the most pleasant and successful she had had with her parents since she could remember. This in itself is to be taken as a sign of progress in separating from her identity as 'daughter' to these powerful parental figures and in placing her relationship to them on a level of greater equality and more balanced reciprocity. All of these facts are assumed and gathered together in the dream and cast in the form of a journey to the land of the dead, where A. experiences the guiding insight for the next steps of her journey through life.

Within the analytic situation, of course, there is another factor —besides the action of Hermes in dreams and synchronistic events —to reckon with, and that is the analyst. The analyst can work either with or against the guiding hand of Hermes: by leading the analysand astray and away from the defenses that guard the corpse, out of fear of what might happen if this were uncovered, on the one hand; or, on the other, by aligning himself with Hermes and moving along this path, as outlined by the unconscious, through the lines of defense to the seat of anxiety and to the basic cause of the psychological impasse in the analysand's present life situation. It seems useful, therefore, that the analyst should learn technique from the insights obtained by observing Hermes, the guide through the lines and the magician who puts the defensive watchmen to sleep. If analytic insight and interpretation are communicated in alignment with the subtle movements of Hermes, they can help the analysand slip past his otherwise vigilant defenses and gain consciousness of what lies "behind the lines" in the unconscious.

The Jungian discussion of this moment in analysis, when the corpse is discovered and the unconscious content is disclosed, would classically center on the "aha" reaction of the analysand to the analyst's interpretation. This reaction implies that an opening has been found through the defenses that have kept a pattern, or an image, or a memory concealed from consciousness. Through careful observance and attention, often in silence, the Hermetic analyst has slipped through the lines and caught sight of the unconscious issue, and if the timing of his insight and interpretation is right, the analysand's ego can come through with him. Then the interpretation is successful in penetrating through the defenses and lifting the guarded unconscious secret into conscious awareness. Such a technique of interpretation does not attack the defenses head-on, and there are no assaults on resistances or efforts to overwhelm the analysand with superior or heroic insight. Rather, there is a stealthy slipping-through movement to the unconscious core of the issue.

In relation to the issue at hand, separation, this kind of interpretation would open access to a well-guarded and concealed self-image or set of identifications that in an earlier phase of development represented an ideal but had since then fallen into unconscious obscurity, where it nevertheless continued to exert a steady but indirect influence on attitudes and behavior. When this set of images and contents is revealed to consciousness, the analysand can recognize the inappropriateness of clinging to them and can finish the separation that was begun earlier. The corpse that has now been located can be brought forward into full awareness, and the necessary ensuing grief reaction can lead to a culmination in burial.

In the first chapter, I defined psychological liminality as the condition in which the ego becomes unmoored from its former fixities of identification and identity and 'floats.' In this chapter I have been making the point that liminality, which is the second phase of the midlife transition, cannot be entered until separation from an earlier pattern of libido-organization, and from its accompanying set of attitudes and its self-consciousness, has been completed. This separation cannot be completed, moreover, until there is a conscious burial of that earlier identity (or *persona*, in the Jungian vocabulary). To say that Hermes facilitates this separation, and therefore that he facilitates the movement into liminality, is to say that the unconscious moves a person in this direction. And as it does so, it moves consciousness closer to an awareness of finitude and death. This movement of consciousness toward the awareness of death produces the well-known and now documented midlife conditions of depression, loss of the 'dream,' death anxiety, and rather obsessive reevaluations of life-goals and ideals. When life is no longer seen from a perspective of beginnings through a fantasy of continuous expansion and growth, but rather from the perspective of ends and of death through a fantasy of fate and limitations, midlife has arrived.

It may seem paradoxical that Hermes, himself a classic *puer* figure, should facilitate this classic *senex* posture, but it must be acknowledged that for the movement backward and downward into this vision of life Hermes is guide. ''The favoring of retrograde movement,'' writes Lopez-Pedraza in his book *Hermes and His*

Children, is an essential Hermes move which "brings about a reconnection to the different complexes, the different parts of one's history and memory" (p. 32). It is this movement back into personal and archetypal memory that brings about the life-review described by so many social scientists who have studied and interviewed persons at midlife, and this, too, is an essential part of the process I refer to as discovering the corpse and burying the dead. Eventually, this retrograde movement brings about the experience of liminality, where fate and destiny become the leading ideas and where notions of possibility and expansion evaporate like illusions.

It goes without saying that these phases of the midlife transition—separation, liminality, and reintegration—cannot be essentially differentiated in life itself, like a neatly trimmed row of discrete boxes through which a person passes cleanly and without residue from one to the next. This three-fold division is a somewhat rough-and-ready distinction within a flowing and often chaotic process, and as I proceed in discussing the phase of liminality it will be plain that separation issues are not completely left behind in it, any more than it is true that the experience of liminality is not a part of the separation phase. Nevertheless, a person is different for having gone *through* the separation phase, because then the psychological attitude of 'floating' can take hold, which is importantly different from the attitude of clinging and holding on that obtains when separation has not been fully assimilated by consciousness.

There is an important difference between 'burying' and 'covering over,' even though both seem equally to put things under ground. When the process of separation is undertaken as a conscious work and fully assimilated and dealt with in its broader ramifications ('burial'), the images that were once unconsciously identified with get converted into objective facts 'out there' and 'then.' Subjective identification is replaced by an objective relation. The point of psychological 'burial' is to effect this conversion. 'Covering over,' on the other hand, does not bring this about. It produces instead self-deception and unconsciousness through repression or denial, and this actually has the effect of prolonging indirect and unconsciously determined subjective identifications. This is what happens in the neurosis of the *puer aeternus*, for example: the *puer*'s identification with the untouched, omnipotent, possible self remains intact through any number of marriages, love affairs, and other obvious challenges to virginal youth, including wrinkles. This prolonged identification rests on the defense of denial, which prevents a true 'burial.' The *puer* self is never converted into an earlier self, which has been lost, mourned, and recognized as a phase of personal history and archetypal experience belonging definitively to the past.

The function of burial, then, is to create separation through this conversion of subjective identifications into objective facts, so that a person can have the kind of relation to them that one has to historical facts. At midlife, this passage through the gate of separation is fraught with fear and with a profound sense of grief for the lost and forever gone image of what one once was.

These feelings stand out in Homer's account of Hektor's burial, which are final lines of the *Iliad*:

Now Priam the aged king spoke forth his word to his people:
"Now, men of Troy, bring timber into the city, and let not
your hearts fear a close ambush of the Argives. Achilleus
promised me, as he sent me on my way from the black ships,
that none should do us injury until the twelfth dawn comes."
    He spoke, and they harnessed to the wagons their mules and
        their oxen
and presently were gathered in front of the city. Nine days
they spent bringing in an endless supply of timber. But when
the tenth dawn had shone forth with her light upon mortals,
they carried out bold Hektor, weeping, and set the body
aloft a towering pyre for burning. And set fire to it.

But when the young dawn showed again with her rosy fingers,
the people gathered around the pyre of illustrious Hektor.
But when all were gathered to one place and assembled
    together,
first with gleaming wine they put out the pyre that was
    burning,
all where the fury of the fire still was in force, and thereafter
the brothers and companions of Hektor gathered the white bones
up, mourning, as the tears swelled and ran down their cheeks.
    Then
they laid what they had gathered up in a golden casket
and wrapped this about with soft robes of purple, and presently
put it away in the hollow of the grave, and over it
piled huge stones laid close together. Lightly and quickly
they piled up the grave-barrow, and on all sides were set
    watchmen
for fear the strong-greaved Achaians might too soon set upon
    them.
They piled up the grave-barrow and went away, and thereafter
assembled in a fair gathering and held a glorious
feast within the house of Priam, king under God's hand.
    Such was their burial of Hektor, breaker of horses.

(24: 777–804)

Chapter Three

Liminality and the Soul

> Gentle, his golden staff gleaming, Hermes appears even among the musty paths of ghosts.
> Kerényi

In the last chapter I discussed the first phase of the midlife transition, separation, by reflecting on the themes of death and burial. One should keep in mind, though, that the phase of separation is still only preliminary to the central experience of the transition, namely, liminality. But it is crucial, I feel, to recognize that liminality is entered through this particular door, through the internal experience of loss and burial of a former sense of self. This earlier sense of identity, which was based on assumptions about who one is in relation to others and was associated with various self-images, ideals, hopes, and expectations, and with a specific remembered past and imagined future, has been left behind.

The entry into the midlife transition, first into the phase of separation and then into liminality, may either come about gradually through many small incremental changes or abruptly through a dramatic shift into an irreversible process of upheaval and change. In either case, though, there is a break in psychological continuity, and the experience of self and others takes on a different—and in liminality a more or less insubstantial and distant—feeling, as though what had formerly been solid now is unreal.

By passing through the experience of separation and coming to terms with a lost past through the act of burial, the soul becomes freed of its attachments to an earlier fixed sense of identity. But initially at least, this freeing of the soul may be expressed symbolically, and experienced, as death or as the fear of death. The familiar phenomenon of death anxiety at midlife is, in addition to the increasing awareness of life's actual limitations, a reflection of this intrapsychic process of disentanglement and disattachment from earlier identifications. This separation from a past identity *is* a death of sorts.

The symbolism of alchemy and of alchemical transformations illustrates this point graphically, that separation is symbolized by death. An important operation in the alchemical *opus* is called *separatio*. Here the soul, which has been enmeshed in matter and attached to a body, is freed from these entanglements. This event of separation is surrounded by imagery of blackness and death and is called the *nigredo* ('blackness') state. Its emotional equivalent is despair, grief, mourning. *Separatio* is an operation intended to prepare the material in the alchemical vessel for the next stage, *unio mentalis*, which is conceived to consist of a union of soul and spirit but separate from the body. Here the alchemists imagined a corpse lying at the bottom of the *vas* and a united soul-and-spirit entity (literally the combination is of water and air) floating above it at the top. Psychologically, this is equivalent to the 'floating' consciousness that is characteristic of liminality: insubstantial, distant from everyday 'facts,' hovering, drifting over the face of the earth. This is to be followed, in turn, by the final step of the process, a reunion of the soul-spirit content with the body, and this union constitutes the mystery of rebirth and rejuvenation (cf. Jung 1970b, §654–789).

The alchemical vessel is, clearly, *both* a tomb and a womb during the period of transformation. And as Victor Turner points out as well, the coalescence of tomb and womb imagery is characteristic of liminality in rites of passage among traditional peoples (1967, p. 99). The death of what has been and the preparation for what will be coexist in liminality. So "death anxiety" is not far from "birth anxiety," an issue not much discussed in the literature on midlife but one certainly as fraught with potential for fearful imagining as the former is filled with dread. What will come of all this? What will become of me? These are wrenching questions as the soul comes free of its attachments and identifications.

A digression. In speaking about the entry into liminality through the door of loss, burial, and separation in the last chapter, I mentioned the issue of timing. Before pursuing further the theme of the soul's being freed in liminality, I want to reflect some more on the issue of timing and to discriminate between two psychological dimensions or kinds of liminality, the synchronic and the diachronic. At certain critical moments in life, the psychological effects of losses or of defeats are greater than they are at other times; they signify more, and they have the effect of 'splitting the block' in a fashion and to a depth that they would not have done at other times. This is not altogether a function of the magnitude of the loss. Sometimes the term of liminality that results from loss and burial is only short-lived, relatively a mere flash of altered consciousness; at other times it takes hold and dominates consciousness for years. Why is this the case?

To this point I have discussed liminality only diachronically, as a segment within a span of time, preceded by the segment *separation* and followed by the segment *reintegration*. Here liminality is viewed as time-bound and clearly limited in duration. But a full discussion of liminality must also see it synchronically, as a permanent dimension or depth of the psyche, a 'layer' that threads through all time and occupies a space in every period of life. At a certain psychological level of things, we are always in liminality, floating and unfixed to identifications, betwixt and between. Liminal figures ("edgemen," as Victor Turner calls them) are always around and present somewhere in the psyche—although a person may not be conscious of their presence or influence and comfortably clothed in well-tailored furnishings and housed in the full paraphernalia of domesticity. This figure appears in dreams as the vagabond, the fool, the outcast, the prophet, the mysterious stranger, the journeyer.

The film-maker Fellini tells a dream in which a liminal figure appears and creates a most impressive effect:

> I am the Director of an airport. A very large plane filled with passengers lands in the middle of the night. I get ready to greet the passengers from behind my table in an immense terminal room with glass walls. Beyond them, I can see lit runways and the large shape of the airplane that has just landed. I get ready to greet the passengers. As the top man in the airport, I also run the Immigration Office. They've all deplaned. Tired from the trip and sitting on benches along the walls, they all wait for me to gesture them over to my table. One of the passengers strikes me more than the others. He's standing over to one side all alone without luggage. When he approaches my table, I notice he's wearing a fancy, worn kimono which gives him a stately, raggedy appearance. Everything about him shows and is, in contrast, like him. [*sic*] The definitely Mongolian Oriental features express great, regal and miserable dignity. It could be the face of an Emperor, of a prophet, of a Saint, but also one of a gypsy, of a wayfarer, of a strolling player who's become indifferent to disdain and suspicion through long habit to mortification and misery. His hands hidden in long sleeves of his kimono, his eyes closed, the foreigner waits my decision in silence. I am overcome by an indefinable feeling. This character fascinates me and communicates a kind of restlessness I cannot control. The other passengers over there say nothing. They're a dark, silent, indistinct mass. The airport terminal is immense. The passenger is motionless, standing straight in front of me with his greasy, dirty hair; with the kind of smell vagabonds have . . . the ugly smell of wet rags, of soaked leaves, of dirt. And, at the same time, with that strange, disturbing, aristocratic glow. He opposes my discomfort and very emotional insecurity with the definite,

inequivocable [*sic*] reality of his arrival and presence. What should I do? The man doesn't speak, doesn't ask for any intervention, doesn't ask questions: he just waits calmly with the confidence of someone identifying himself with an unavoidable event of destiny. It's true. The circumstance doesn't concern him, it concerns me. I'm the one who must decide if he can enter or not. He did what he had to do. Now it's up to me. All he had to do was to arrive and now he's here. The suspicion that the situation is so inevitable increases my discomfort, my state of malaise. I stammer some hypocritical excuses, heat up assuring him I'm not really the Airport Director and the decision doesn't depend on me. It depends on other, more competent, more important people. I stall, try to avoid the situation, keep coming up with justifications and childish lies which are less and less convincing. I'm more and more embarrassed until I become silent, seized by a confused, suspended feeling of shame. A great silence falls on everything. I feel as if so much time had gone by . . . the unreachable, impenetrable, dusty and gleaming Oriental is still there in front of me, waiting. But for how long? I've lowered my head and stare at the little rectangular plaque on my desk with the words "THE DIREC-TOR" on it with a discomfortable [*sic*] feeling of ironic self-pity. Are the others still there? And the mysterious passenger from the Orient? Is he still waiting? I don't dare raise my head and slowly form this thought: what am I afraid of if I do raise my eyes? To find the foreigner still there or not to find him at all anymore?

The 'ghost' or 'shade' in a dream is, similarly, a figure representative of liminality, as in the dream I recounted in the last chapter, where the dreamer found herself being embraced by a young woman and suddenly realized the woman was in fact dead. Because liminality exists as a dimension or a domain within the psyche, liminal figures of this kind can appear in dreams at any time during life, not only during major transitional periods.

At midlife a person runs into a period when the liminality that is produced by external facts such as aging, loss of loved ones, or the failure to attain a dream of youthful ambition combines with the liminality that is generated internally by independently shifting in-trapsychic structures, and the result is an intense and prolonged ex-perience of liminality, one that often endures for years. At this point, diachronic and synchronic liminality come together syn-chronistically. "Synchronism" is defined in *Webster's Third Inter-national Dictionary* with an image that aptly portrays this kind of cooperation of forces: it is "the condition of excessive rolling obtain-ing where a ship's rolling period is equal to the wave period or to one half the wave period." When these two motions coincide in this pattern of cooperation, the ship's natural roll becomes excessive. This is midlife liminality. Always the ship is rolling, and always some liminality is present within the psyche. Always, too, the sea is rolling: life throws up crises and failures that prove our limitations all the time. But when these two motions get together, and the force of each is great enough, they produce a degree of rolling that can reach excessive proportions. In this excessive rolling, through an in-tense and prolonged experience of liminality, the Hermetic attitude and the presence of Hermes are particularly welcome and valuable. Whatever we can learn from Hermes, it will serve us best when the experience of liminality is deep and excessive and when it threatens to capsize our vessels into a severely disturbed sea.

Both "diachronic" and "synchronic" ('through time' and 'with time') contain an embedded reference to *chronos* ('time'). We do liminality—and Hermes too for that matter—an injustice if not out-right violence by limiting discussion of them to the perspective of *chronos*, if we understand time only in the linear sense, diachron-ically. Turner observes that the experience of liminality includes an altered sense of time, "in and out of time," as he puts it (1969, p. 96). Liminality, so frequently and classically imaged as wander-ings in the desert (cf. J. Stein, p. 276), contains a different experience of time from that of ordinary diurnal ego-consciousness. When the Bible says that the Hebrews wandered in the wilderness for forty years, we should read it as "for an indefinitely and critically long period of time, forever.'' ''Forty years'' means 'forever,' as in 'it went on forever.' This is metaphorical language, and it contains the expanded spaces of indefiniteness that imagination can fill. But the text of the Bible is arranged diachronically—the redactors of the Bible were not in liminality, even if the original authors and creators of its religion most probably were—so metaphors like this tend, understandably enough, to be taken literally. Diachronic literalism cannot understand Hermetic liminality because it has no empathy for it.

Diachronic schemas tend to arrange events in a linear sequence: first this, then that, a progression of events through time. And these events, in turn, tend to get placed into patterns that are perceived through the notion of causation: not only 'first this, then that,' but 'that *because of* this first.' When this perspective rules psychological understanding, we get life as a developmental sequence of steps and stages, earlier ones causing (or leading to) later ones, later ones building on or failing because of earlier ones, etc. A psychology of liminality written from the diachronic perspective, such as Erik Erikson's discussion of the ''moratorium'' period during identity formation, yields a kind of avuncular view of it, an objective impression, quite different from the experience itself and from a psychological discussion of liminality that ensues when it is discussed from within the experience of liminality itself. (An instance of this is James Hillman's *The Dream and the Underworld*.) Liminal memory patterns are different from diachronic ones. Times and events fall together differently. Identity, too, and the multitude of imprints, experiences, fixations, and identifications contained within it are rearranged on a skein of different values and valences. New things stand out, familiar images recede, the landscape buckles and twists.

So far in these pages I have discussed midlife liminality within the context of a diachronic framework, using the schema van Gennep applied to rites of passage: first separation, then liminality, and finally reintegration. This framing gives definition to and puts boundaries on this discussion of liminality, and one of its subtle purposes may be to avoid the anxiety of not being able to hold or to contain this elusive subject. Nevertheless, I have done this knowing that this frame cannot contain the portrait of either psychological liminality or the figure of Hermes. Both of these exist precisely outside of, or beside, all diachronic domains; they thread through and around them and end up eluding the grasp of their borders. Hermes is quicksilver and cannot be fixed in thought-containers that are alien to his own mercurial ways. Similarly, the experience of midlife liminality cannot be adequately portrayed in diachronic terms alone. Like the unconscious itself, which in part resists being boxed into fixed temporal contexts and causal sequences but always keeps to itself a measure of freedom to float and to drift, to pass through the keyholes of the psychological shelters we construct, Hermes and liminality appear surprisingly and unexpectedly in the forms of dreams, fantasies, and synchronistic events. While Chronos-controlled consciousness seeks to fix these and box them in, Hermes and the world of liminality slip past its control points and hasten away, remaining elusive.

Is there a more Hermetic method, then, that might be up to the job of elucidating midlife liminality and conveying its quality and meaning? Perhaps we should free our method, like liminality frees the soul, from the strictures of systematic order and diachronic progressions and move Hermetically instead by floating freely, by associative wandering, by apercu, by backtracking and rhetorical repetition, by stealth and thievery. Brainstorms, insights, lucky finds, intuitions, the play of dreams—if these are threaded together and held somewhat loosely in hand, will we not have a style that belongs to Hermes rather than to grandfather Chronos (or to brother Apollo)? But will this method 'produce,' or will it like Hermes who "beguiles endlessly the tribes of mortal men throughout the night" (*Hymn*, 577–78) deceive us into thinking we have a result, some *thing* to hold on to, to take away and apply, when in fact the gain is liable to evaporate with the turning of a page or the closing of this book, leaving us empty-handed and confused? If we are deceived in this way, however, it is a taste of liminality itself and also authentically Hermetic. To be beguiled into thinking there is something solid where there are actually only mirages and insubstantial vapors resembles the experience we are trying to explore and depict. So if this is the result, it will be a true picture of liminality. When people come out of midlife liminality and think back on it, they may not believe it really happened. It has the quality of dreams.

There is one additional feature to this Hermetic method, however, and this must be recognized and consciously incorporated if the method is to be exploited to greatest advantage. This pertains to what is done with the lucky find, the thieved thought, the sudden psychological insight once it is in hand, and to the attitude that informs this action. Hermes is not just a collector, and the Hermetic method, if true to its master practitioner, cannot simply pile up random collections of interesting and loosely related observations. The 'find' must be taken up and craftily transformed in a characteristically Hermetic manner. The *Hymn to Hermes* illustrates the nature of this transformational act and attitude. So essentially does this belong to the archetypal pattern Hermes represents, on which this method rests, that this episode is the very first recounted about this impish infant son of Zeus and Maia:

> After he sprang forth from his mother's immortal limbs,
> he did not remain for long lying in his holy cradle,
> but he leaped up and searched for the cattle of Apollon,
> stepping over the threshold of the high-roofed cave.
> There he found a tortoise and won boundless bliss,
> for Hermes was the first to make a singer of a tortoise,
> which met him at the gates of the courtyard,
> grazing on the lush grass near the dwelling
> and dragging its straddling feet; and the helpful son of Zeus

laughed when he saw it and straightway he said:
"Already an omen of great luck! I don't despise you.
Hail, O shapely hoofer and companion of the feast!
Your sight is welcome! Whence this lovely toy,
the gleaming shell that clothes you, a tortoise living on the
    mountains?
But I shall take you and bring you inside; you'll profit me.
And I shall not dishonor you for you will serve me first.
Better to be inside; being at the gates is harmful for you.
Indeed alive you shall be a charm against baneful
witchcraft; and if you die, your singing could be beautiful."
Thus he spoke and with both hands he raised it up
and ran back into his abode, carrying the lovely toy.
There he tossed it upside down and with a chisel of gray iron
he scooped out the life of the mountain-turtle.
As when swift thought pierces the breast
of a man in whom thick-coming cares churn,
or as when flashing glances dart from quick-rolling eyes,
so glorious Hermes pondered word and deed at once.
He cut measured stalks of reed and fastened them on
by piercing through the back the shell of the tortoise;
and skillfully he stretched oxhide round the shell
and on it he fixed two arms joined by a crosspiece
from which he stretched seven harmonious strings of sheep-gut.
And when it was finished, he held up the lovely toy
and with the plectron struck it tunefully, and under his hand
the lyre rang awesome.

(Hymn, 20–54)

Kerényi's comments on this episode in the *Hymn* deserve more
than just a passing reference; in them he elucidates the essence of
the attitude with which this step of the Hermetic method is undertaken:

Here it is not "the luck-bringing son of Zeus" who laughs, speaks, and acts, but rather the "swift as death son of Zeus". . . . The irony of his words springs from his divinity and is as merciless as Being itself. It is based on "seeing through." Seeing through is divine. Greek tragedy offers its spectators a divine standpoint in that it allows them to participate in such a penetrating vision. . . . In the same way Hermes "sees through" the tortoise. There is no doubt what he sees there. He names the unsociable beast with an expression that alludes to a divinely established designation of the lyre, "friend of the feast." He sees already the glorious instrument while the poor tortoise is still alive. For the tortoise, that glory means a painful death. If the "through-seer" of such a fate is God, he makes light of the irony of the situation that is visible only to him. But it is Titanically cruel-hearted if he bursts out laughing at what he sees, if his words make that irony dazzinly [sic] manifest and if his violent deed helps to fulfill that destiny. This is what Hermes does, not naively, but roguishly and without compassion. (1976, p. 26)

Hermes' attitude, as depicted in the *Hymn* and expounded by Kerényi, is ironic and pragmatic. He is the unsentimental through-seer who glimpses an outrageous possibility and is not constrained from realizing it. This is an attitude inherent in the atmosphere of liminality itself. It is characteristic of "edgemen," who exist outside the accepted assumptions of society and collective opinion, clownish and ironic as they play the Fool and often cruel in creating lucky breaks out of chance encounters. The method demands that this figure and the attitude he represents cue us as we enter and pass through this discussion of liminality. Hermes, the liminal figure par excellence, who corresponds to the liminal potential in each of us, bestows the capacity for seeing through pretensions and facades, since he is himself so unpretentious and unattached to persona and facade. This is where we stand and how we see when we are in liminality. Persona is *mere* persona, only a hollow mask full of lies and preposterous posturing, to be ridiculed and mocked, as the soul looks out from its position of submersion in the depths of liminal experience.*

Hermes does not yet possess a persona. He is unknown, a new wild thing in the world, without a position in social structure and hierarchy, outside of the standardized ways of thinking, feeling, and behaving, and not yet influenced by conditioning and learning. In this sense he *is* naive. So from the edge he pierces through appearances and fixed positions to novel possibilities for transformation and advantage. And he has the imagination and energy for pragmatic assertions of will and thought that the collectivized person would not see or could not perform.

In using the Hermetic method to gain insight and to find guidance through the midlife experience of liminality, therefore, we must seize the observations, images, and thoughts that come along, from wherever they may happen to come, with the playful but unsentimental attitude that is characteristic of Hermes, and bend them to our theme, an end perhaps not foreseen or intended by their own 'natures.' Could the painfully introverted little turtle have guessed that, transformed, he would become the life of the party?

This method of research and exploration is, of course, vastly different from the quantitative and qualitative research methods used by contemporary social scientists to study the midlife transition, although it may pick up and use some of their findings. The goal of those methods is to find and establish statistically valid generalizations or somewhat general truths. For that the Hermetic method is less than useful; it would be ludicrous. Its goal is not to establish facts but to interpret them. As an interpretive method, the Her-

* It should be noted that when Jung discussed the persona most definitively and classically, in "The Structure of the Unconscious" (dated 1916), which became the second of the *Two Essays in Analytical Psychology*, and wrote that it is "only the mask worn by the collective psyche, a mask that *feigns individuality*" (*CW* 7, §465), he was himself deeply immersed in his own midlife transition and was experiencing intense liminality, as his autobiography testifies.

metic method is closer to, but still quite other than, the conventional humanistic method, which relies on the systematic examination and comparison of texts relevant to a topic. Jung's preferred method, amplification, is a variation of the humanistic method.

Like the methods of the social sciences, the Hermetic method *is* empirical, in that it begins with and constantly adverts to 'facts,' but for the collection of data relevant for the discussion of these facts it relies largely on loose associations and synchronistic occurrences ('finds'), and then it employs craftiness and even what might be called distortions in working over these materials and transforming them to its own ends. The test of this method must be strictly pragmatic—is the interpretation that results from it *useful* because it succeeds in portraying the quality and the dimensions of midlife liminality and in elucidating its meanings? or is it too idiosyncratic and therefore without cash value to anyone but perhaps the user of it?

Leaving behind this digression on the timing of major periods of liminality and on Hermetic method, I turn back now to the main theme of this chapter, the freeing of the soul in the experience of liminality at midlife. The imagery of liminal experience, and of the entry into a major epoch of it, is archetypal. It will be recognized as the imaginal equivalent of the emotional experience of liminality by anyone who has traveled this way. There is an epiphany of Hermes at the opening of the Twenty-Fourth Book of the *Odyssey* that supplies a classic example of the imagery typical of the entry into the depths of liminal existence. This Book opens just after the suitors have been killed by Odysseus. These rather unappealing men have been thrown into a radical experience of liminality, having just experienced one of life's major defeats, namely, the sudden loss of life itself. But for the moment their souls are 'betwixt and between' this plane of existence and the next, in a kind of double liminality: they exist on a borderline between this world and the underworld to which they are destined. From this threshold, Hermes will lead them down winding corridors into the very depths of liminal existence itself, the house of Hades. The imagery of this passage into liminality is characteristic and evocative of the experience to come:

> Hermes of Kyllene summoned the souls of the suitors
> to come forth, and in his hands he was holding the beautiful
> golden staff, with which he mazes the eyes of those mortals
> whose eyes he would maze, or wakes again the sleepers.
> Herding
> them on with this, he led them along, and they followed,
> gibbering.
> And as when bats in the depth of an awful cave flitter
> and gibber, when one of them has fallen out of his place in
> the chain that the bats have formed by holding one on another;
> so, gibbering, they went their way together, and Hermes
> the kindly healer led them along down moldering pathways.
> They went along, and passed the Ocean stream, and the White
> Rock,
> and passed the gates of Helios the Sun, and the country
> of dreams, and presently arrived in the meadow of asphodel.
> This is the dwelling place of souls, images of dead men.
>
> (24: 1–14)

The imagery is graphic and stunning: a dark passage along moldering pathways through caves, chains of bats breaking and fluttering in panic, to a place of pure souls where there exist only "images of dead men." When these newly released souls, the suitors, arrive, they come in on a discussion that is being carried on among these "images of dead men" who were the heroes of the Trojan war. Achilleus and Agamemnon are remembering their lives, and Agamemnon complains about his dishonorable wife who slew him in his own home after he had survived the battlefields at Troy. Then the suitors arrive and tell of another woman's treachery, Penelope's, but Agamemnon praises her while again cursing his own wife's infidelity. Here are souls stripped of bodies, remembering their lives and reflecting (albeit bitterly) on the human condition, on some success but mostly on defeat; on matters of honor and deceit, virtue and treachery, fidelity and betrayal. One of the sources of their bitterness is that these complaints and observations are voiced within a context of irreversible finality: nothing can be done about any of it. The time for doing is past, and now memories flood in, and one can only remember and reflect. No other future than this one, bitter as it is, can be imagined. The soul freed from waking physical existence enters a fantasy of permanent liminality.

To be in true liminality, or in liminality truly, however, *is* to be in it for keeps. This belongs to the nature of the experience. It is absolute, and there is no way back to pre-liminal existence. The soul senses that this passage is one-way and that this condition will endure through all time, or until perhaps it fades away. It is in this condition of seemingly permanent liminality, too, that Hermes is guide and can be a teacher. As the archetypal edgeman, he exists in these borderline conditions all the time and is at home in them. For this reason, he is the guide of souls: Hermes escorts the souls of the suitors to "the dwelling place of souls, images of dead men." And what takes place there, in this men's group, is soul-talk.

In *The Origins of European Thought*, Onians presents a fascinating discussion of the ancient Greek notion of *psyché*, one of the Greek words for "soul." The *psyché*, he writes, is to be distinguished from the "breath-soul," which exists in the lungs and diaphragm and expires or is shattered at death. *Psyché*, on the other hand, is akin to our notion of a life-force, and it persists after death in the underworld as a "shade" or "shadow" or as an *eidolon*, "image." This soul, the *psyché*, is located in the head. I will take, Hermetically, a short passage from Onians and conclude this chapter by turning it to my theme of freeing the soul in midlife liminality:

For Pindar the *áiownos* *éidolon* ['immortal image'] (= *psyché*), which "alone comes from the gods" and survives death, "sleeps while the limbs are active, but, to those that sleep, in many a dream it shows decision of things delightful and grievous creeping on." So too in Homer the *psyché* apparently has no part in ordinary waking life and might well be thought to be resident in the head, the contents of which, unlike those of the breast, also seem not to move in ordinary waking life. It may be significant that alike the dream-spirit (*óneiros*), the *psyché* of the dead, and the god appearing to a man in sleep are described as standing not at the side nor at the feet, but, in all the seven passages in point, at or above the head of the recumbent sleeper. (Pp. 102–03)

One thing this passage suggests in connection with our discussion of liminality at midlife is that in liminality the soul not only comes free but also awake. This aspect of our being, the psyche, which usually goes unnoticed and slumbers while we are busy and active and appears only in dreams, comes free and fully awake during liminality. Through defeat and death, we become awake to soul because our other modes of consciousness have ceased functioning. The soul becomes detached from the solid body of the ego's identifications, and Hermes, who represents the leading and guiding function of the unconscious, conducts awareness into a region where subjectivity is not only reality but the *only* reality. Here souls are vivid images, and they commune with one another, commiserating and reflecting on existence. Hermes, then, is the guide to psychic existence, and liminality, to which he leads at midlife, is the realm of soul.

If we reflect on the psychological purpose of the midlife transition and of the experience of prolonged and intense liminality during it, one outstanding point seems to be that it brings about a new kind of self-awareness, namely, consciousness of what is otherwise perhaps sensed, but only vaguely, as the tacit background of waking life, "the unconscious." In liminality a person has the chance to realize he is a self, a soul, and not only a function, an ego. In Jungian terms, this is awareness of the unconscious itself, and it leads to a sense of the foundations upon which consciousness rests, the archetypal dimensions of psychological reality. Ultimately, this can lead to consciousness of a non-egoic Self that plays through all experience though usually perceived only dimly, if at all, and even denied in the seeming brilliance, but actual becloudedness, of purely egoic self-perception. At midlife, through the experience of liminality, the soul is freed from this self-delusion and awakens to a level that endures beyond the ego's defeat and death.

Chapter Four

The Return of the Repressed
during Midlife Liminality

> But Want of Money and the Distress of A
> Thief can never be alledged as the Cause of his
> Thievery. for many honest people endure
> greater hard ships with Fortitude We must
> therefore seek the Cause elsewhere than in want
> of Money for that is the Misers passion, not the
> Thiefs
>
> William Blake

I take up the next thread in these Hermetic reflections on midlife liminality by considering some sentences from Norman O. Brown's book, *Hermes the Thief*. Brown, a classicist, points out that in "the Greek language the characteristic terms applied to Hermes as thief are derivatives of *kléptein*, which in fifth-century Athens meant what 'theft' means to us. But in Homeric Greek the root had two well-established meanings: 'to remove secretly' and, more frequently, 'to deceive'" (p. 10). Brown also observes that "the only ritual which enacted the behavior of the god was the one performed at the festival of Hermes at Samos, at which there was general license to *steal* (*kléptein*)" (p. 6). And, finally, he comments on the verb *kléptein* as follows: "The root *kléptein*, which, with the root *dolos*, furnishes the characteristic terms for Hermes the Trickster and, later, Hermes the Thief, throws further light on the primitive concept of magic. Its original meaning was 'secret action.' To the primitive mind 'secret action' means magic" (p. 19).

Reading through Brown's text, with its frequent repetition of the Greek word for thieving, *kléptein*, and his emphasis on Hermes as *thief*, led me to consider a pathological possibility for the expression of this archetype during the midlife transition and liminality, namely, kleptomania, the mania (or compulsion) for thieving. Could it be that Hermes is behind this form of psychopathology? Is kleptomania a disguised epiphany of Hermes? And if so, supposing this kind of pathology happens to appear during midlife liminality, what does it mean?

But before tackling these questions, what does it mean to say that a 'god' is 'in' or 'behind' an emotional reaction or a pattern of behavior? Before this idea can be useful, the theoretical position on which it rests needs to be understood. In his "Commentary on 'The Secret of the Golden Flower,'" published in 1929, Jung makes a statement that sums up the theoretical backing for an archetypal interpretation of psychopathology:

> We think we can congratulate ourselves on having already reached such a pinnacle of clarity, imagining that we have left all these phantasmal gods far behind. But what we have left behind are only verbal spectres, not the psychic facts that were responsible for the birth of the gods. We are still as much possessed by autonomous psychic contents as if they were Olympians. Today they are called phobias, obsessions, and so forth; in a word, neurotic symptoms. The gods have become diseases; Zeus no longer rules Olympus but rather the solar plexus, and produces curious specimens for the doctor's consulting room, or disorders the brains of politicians and journalists who unwittingly let loose psychic epidemics on the world. (1967, §54)

These lines, which were put to paper several years before the German Nazis unleashed their own brand of psychopathology on the world, summarize a great deal of earlier theorizing. In a nutshell, the idea is that the unconscious psychological contents and dynamics that once created images of gods and mythic events have not disappeared with the waning of religious belief but continue to affect human consciousness, only now in the forms of neurosis and psychopathology. In short, the gods now reveal themselves in diseases and symptoms. From this it follows that insight and therapy would be greatly enhanced by knowing the correspondences between mythic patterns and psychopathological symptoms. This should offer essential clues as to what these disturbances signify.

To the question of what it signifies when an archetype appears as a psychopathological symptom, Jung offers a key suggestion in what is perhaps his most concise and articulate paper on the relation of psyche and myth, "The Psychology of the Child Archetype":

> Archetypes were, and still are, living psychic forces that demand to be taken seriously, and they have a strange way of making sure of their effect. Always they were the bringers of protection and salvation, and their violation has as its consequence the "perils of the soul" known to us from the psychology of primitives. Moreover, they are the unfailing causes of neurotic and even psychotic disorders, behaving exactly like neglected or maltreated physical organs or organic functional systems. (1959a, §266)

The key point here, and the one I will develop in the remainder of this chapter, is that psychopathological symptoms are manifestations of "neglected archetypes." From this it follows that the 'cure' for psychopathological symptoms includes remedying this state of neglect, and this means discovering which archetype ('god') has been neglected and then 'honoring' it. If we study kleptomania carefully and follow the movement of Hermes within this irrational pattern of behavior, the symptom should lead us to the archetype that has been neglected ('repressed') and is now insisting on restitution by possessing the ego. During midlife liminality, we often find the surprising appearance of such puzzling pathological symptoms, and these, if we learn to read their meanings, can tell us what has been repressed and neglected by virtue of the requirements and restrictions laid down by the earlier development of a dominant pattern of libido-organization that had the effect of splitting the psyche and excluding expression of certain portions of it.

The following example illustrates the principle that archetypes reveal themselves as ego-possession and that this psychopathological symptom can be cured by taking a religious attitude toward the archetype motivating it. Laurel Kendall, a Western-trained anthropologist and student of Korean shamanism, in an article entitled "Suspect Saviors of Korean Hearths and Homes," described an instance of possession as a "shamanic call":

> Outcast and official appointee, suspected charlatan and possible savior, the shaman is herself ambivalent about her calling from the start. She begins her professional life struggling against the gods. Her suffering and tortured resistance, which testify to the veracity of the call, enhance her legitimacy. No woman wants to become a shaman, but, the women say, those who refuse the will of the gods die raving lunatics.
>
> The gods descend into a destined shaman and lead her to strange, wild behavior. Initiation as a shaman is the only possible solution. An established shaman organizes an initiation kut. Once initiated, the new shaman controls the onset of her visions and can divine with coins and rice grains. Women crowd into her home to test her powers. Some acquire renown, a vast clientele, and a bit of wealth. People remember them as "great shamans" long after their deaths. . . .
>
> . . . Yongsu's Mother (as she is called in the village) . . . invited me to a number of kut and patiently explained the lore of gods and ghosts throughout my fieldwork. An ideal informant, she was perceptive, articulate, and uniquely self-reliant in a society where a woman alone has few recourses. Her life history ran like a melodrama.
>
> Widowed after two years of marriage, she was left with two stepchildren and her own small son. She worked as a peddler, one of the limited number of occupations open to a woman supporting a family. At the end of the mourning period, she went to an older shaman's kut.

When the village women donned the shaman's costumes and danced to amuse their personal gods and give their families good fortune, the shaman urged Yongsu's Mother to dance for success in her precarious business ventures.

> *So I put on the robes, and right away I was dancing wildly. I ran into the shrine, still dancing, and grabbed the Spirit Warrior's flags. . . . I demanded money. All of the women gave me money. I ran all the way home. My heart was thumping wildly. I just wanted to die like a crazy woman. Later, we talked about it this way and that way and decided there was no way out. So, the next year, I was initiated as a mansin.*

Now a veteran of 7 years, Yongsu's Mother, who is 40 years old, earns a full-time living as a shaman. Her warmth and mischievous humor make her house a favorite gathering place for village women, many of whom have become regular clients. (P. 46)

Here we see how, in 'primitive' circumstances, a psychopathological state is treated through an archetypal interpretation; the cure is effected through finding the meaning of symptoms and taking a religious attitude toward the archetypal content behind them. In this way, the psyche is honored, and the ego is released from its state of possession.

The modern psychotherapist gives recognition to the 'god' in a symptom by interpreting it archetypally. The therapist makes this kind of an interpretation by using the method of amplification, which brings an individual's personal psychological material (symptoms) into association with a relevant archetypal (usually mythical) figure or motif. But finding the relevant myth is only the first step in this hermeneutic. The second exposes what Jung calls the "unconscious core of meaning" underlying both symptom and myth (cf. 1959a, §266). The statement of this "core of meaning" is necessarily inexhaustive and partial but, if adequate, it constitutes an intelligible and psychologically relevant restatement of the archetype from which both the set of symptoms and the mythic image derive.

It is important to recognize that it is this core of psychological mean-ing, not the mythic amplification, that is the 'god' we are seeking.

An interpretation is completed when this restated core of mean-ing is brought back and applied to the individual's current life situa-tion. This move completes the "hermeneutic circle." The Jungian analyst performs this final step, typically, by using the principle of compensation, which states that the unconscious core of meaning (the 'god') stands in a compensatory relation to the one-sidedness of consciousness and has a teleological function: namely, to address a critical deficit within the position of ego-consciousness and to show what is needed for its remedy.

This third step in interpretation raises the question of this method's psychotherapeutic potential. The interpreter-healer in a traditional culture might say something like this to his 'patient': "These symptoms are signs that the such-and-such god is displeased and feels forgotten. Go to this god and pay homage; make a sacrifice; perform acts of worship. Consult the god about what it is you are to do next." Perhaps this would lead the patient to become initiated in-to a cult or into a god's service as a priest or devotee. The modern psychotherapist, on the other hand, might say, or imply, something like this to his patient: "Your symptoms indicate developmental deficits and a one-sided attitude of consciousness that neglect (or repress) important parts of the Self; this is what lies behind your neurotic symptoms (or psychotic possession). Your symptoms are actually attempts on the part of the psyche to heal you, to bring about greater psychological integration and wholeness. You should be grateful for them because they tell you what you need to attend to for your own individuation." By opening the patient's ego-consciousness to the unconscious and by attending to the neglected archetype, the therapeutic interpreter would proceed to attempt clearing the path for the self-regulative processes of the psyche to work and to contribute their healing effects.

To make this kind of interpretation and carry it out in therapeutic practice, the psychotherapist obviously needs to be familiar with mythic patterns and figures. The "unconscious core of meaning" cannot be revealed at this level unless the contents and dynamics of the collective unconscious are understood and taken into account. An archetypal interpretation places a symptom in the realm of religious disorder, and this in itself already lends the symptom a degree of meaning it would not otherwise have: one of the archetypes ('gods') is demanding attention and calling the soul to its attendance and service. This kind of interpretation calls forth a religious attitude in the sufferer, in the sense that Jung defined the religious attitude as "a careful consideration and observation of certain dynamic factors that are conceived as 'powers': spirits, daemons, gods, laws, ideas, ideals, or whatever name man has given to such factors in his world as he has found powerful, dangerous, or helpful enough to be taken into careful consideration, or grand, beautiful and meaningful enough to be devoutly worshipped and loved" (1963, §8). The *homo religiosus* is, for Jung, "the man who takes into account and carefully observes certain factors which influence him and his general condition" (ibid., §11). This is the attitude toward the psychological reasons underlying symptoms that this type of interpretation aims to create in a patient.

This is the outline of the interpretive method I will use in the following reflections on the psychopathological symptom known in the psychiatric nomenclature as kleptomania.

The Harvard Guide to Modern Psychiatry classifies kleptomania as one of the "Impulse Disorders." Alfred Stanton, the author of the *Guide*'s article on personality disorders, offers a description of the typical symptoms: "Patients with impulse disorders recurrently carry out complex stereotyped actions, usually clearly antisocial, often with a great though obscure excitement and fear of being caught, for reasons they are generally at a loss to explain" (p. 291).

Persons suffering from this form of psychopathology are clearly in the grip of an unconscious (to them) content and dynamic when they enact their curious dramas. The fact that their actions are stereotyped and highly predictable indicates the presence of an underlying structure of fantasy and action, an unconsciously determined "pattern of behavior." The great excitement they feel is of obscure origin and meaning, indicating unconscious sources of libido. And that the reasons for their enactments are wholly obscure to themselves indicates an unconscious center of control and power. Primitives would certainly consider persons in this psychological state to be possessed by spirits and under obligation to carry out their instructions and injunctions with ritualistic order and precision. Excitement and enthusiasm indicate the presence of 'demons' or 'gods.'

Stanton, in his modern textbook analysis, continues: "Like the compulsive person who 'cannot' stop touching a doorknob, biting his fingernails, or touching a part of his body, the impulse-disordered patient wonders why he must do the things he does, makes resolutions, notes with despair the risks he is taking, and continues to take them" (ibid., pp. 291–92). Clearly this person must be in the grip of something greater, or at least more psychologically powerful, than his ego. This "something greater" is one of those "dynamic factors that are conceived as 'powers'" described by Jung (1963, §8) in his discussion of archetypes.

Kleptomania is one of several impulse disorders, which the *Harvard Guide* lists as follows: transvestitism (a disorder that manifests itself in the compulsion to wear clothing of the opposite sex and to present oneself as a member of that sex; to reverse sexual identity), voyeurism (the compulsion secretly to watch other people in intimate acts, such as undressing, having sexual intercourse, etc.), exhibitionism (the compulsion to show off one's genitals in public), pyromania (the compulsion to stimulate sexual arousal by lighting fires and watching them burn), compulsive gambling, polydrug addiction, and compulsive spending. All of these are disorders in what must be considered 'normal' human impulses. It is the compulsiveness, the obscurity of motivation, and the general unconsciousness of these behaviors that mark them as pathological. It is a striking thought that each of these disorders could be associated to the mythic pattern of Hermes and profitably insighted through the use of this figure. Perhaps the archetype underlying the image of Hermes makes an appearance in *all* impulse disorders. But this is quintessentially true for kleptomania, since Hermes is so intimately linked in myth with the act of thieving.

Kleptomania, an impulse *disorder*, is a disorder within a normal impulse. The impulse to steal is not itself a disorder: everyone feels it at one time or another, and while it may be antisocial, it cannot be considered inherently aberrant or psychopathological. It belongs to human nature. Because this impulse *is* a normal part of human makeup, backed by an archetype and represented in archetypal images, stealing is much more ubiquitous among human beings than is the fairly rare pathological variant of it, kleptomania. The universality of the impulse makes it necessary to have a Commandment against it, to protect the social order and the individuals in society from the undermining effects that would result if this impulse were indulged on a collective scale. It is obvious that if this impulse were not a universally human one there would be no need for the existence, in all societies, of laws against it.

Also helpful for the understanding of kleptomania is seeing it in contrast to such character disorders as psychopathy and sociopathy. Where thieving arises from the impulse disorder kleptomania, persons feel an internal prohibition against stealing: the act is known and felt to be wrong, and these persons feel guilty for acting on the impulse. In the character disorders, on the other hand, where the prohibition against stealing is felt to be external to the self, individuals feel no guilt or remorse for acting on the impulse to steal. It is evident, therefore, that the internal psychological structures of the kleptomaniac are more complex than are those of the sociopathic thief, who simply acts on impulse without regard for others or for the general welfare.

Where the impulse to steal appears without complication and in its normal form, as the wish to take something without paying for it or bargaining for it, it is not difficult to make out motives: they are more or less transparent, and the goal of the act is quite concrete. The impulse, moreover, remains under ego-control, so the law legitimately holds us accountable for acting on the wish to steal. But kleptomania is a *mania* for stealing, and the impulse to steal is so charged with energy that the ego is rendered nearly helpless and often cannot resist it. It is much more questionable to hold persons suffering from this condition accountable for their thieving actions. Also, where kleptomania rules, the goal of stealing is not all too clear. This maniacal passion for stealing is altogether different from stealing because one wants something but does not have the money to buy it. Where *thieving itself* is constellated in the psyche as an ir-resistible impulse, it is immaterial whether one could buy the thing or not; it must be taken by theft and not by some other means. The object itself is often even trivial, its value largely symbolic rather than monetary.

So the psychological questions are: why is the psyche constellated in this fashion? what is the developmental deficit and one-sidedness of ego-consciousness that this disorder is a pathological attempt to compensate? how should we understand the aims of this curious form of psychological self-treatment, particularly when it occurs during midlife liminality?

I take the view that episodic kleptomania at midlife is an epiphany of Hermes. An archetype of the unconscious is asserting a powerful counterwill in the form of compulsive thieving, and the ego is overwhelmed by this force and confused as to its meaning and obscure intention.

A middle-aged woman who came into my analytical practice with what was ostensibly a marriage problem reported that she had been afflicted in the last year with an unmanageable compulsion to steal small articles from cosmetics counters in dime stores. Married to a prominent member of the community in which she lived and the mother of several 'fine children,' she was more than a little embarrassed and ashamed of this bizarre behavior and lived in terror of being caught. She could not understand what came over her and why she had to steal items that she could easily afford to buy if she wanted them.

She was herself the product of a rigorous religious upbringing and commitment. Her devotion had in recent years waned, however, as her husband had pulled away from her and indeed had begun showing a persistent and more than troublesome interest in another woman. Her mothering function had changed radically, too, as her children had grown up and had become independent and autonomous. Her importance within the family, and its support of her, had diminished, and so it was not surprising that her sense of self-esteem, which had rested largely on being 'good'—i.e., on putting herself and her own wishes last, after husband and his career, after children and their needs, after parents and in-laws, etc.—was crumbling. She felt the foundations and root assumptions of her life giving away.

This woman's former dominant pattern of self-organization as wife and mother, and the identity and self-esteem based on it, was being threatened. This came at a time in her life, moreover, when other more internal intrapsychic changes were taking place as well, and these were joining forces and helping to 'split the block' and to create a state of midlife liminality. When she came to see me, she had been in this condition for roughly a year, and she wanted help in patching things back together.

Thieving introduced a compulsive and unconsciously determined set of actions into this woman's life. Her acts of theft originated in a repressed piece of her personality (in Jungian terminology, the "shadow"), and in these kleptomaniacal episodes this piece was returning to her behavioral repertoire. But the peculiar and indirect way in which it expressed itself made it nearly impossible for her to understand what it was and what it demanded. Consciously, this woman did not know what she was doing or why.

It is almost predictable that the repressed shadow will return at midlife and particularly during midlife liminality. 'Adolescent' is often the feeling described as accompanying its return: "I feel like a teenager again." Perhaps because the structures of defense against the unconscious are less able to hold the repressed contents out, or because the unconscious is more strongly charged with energy than usual and is able to break through them, or a combination of these two reasons, the impulses, drives, fantasies, longings, and wishes that were previously repressed make a powerful reappearance during midlife. And one of the many forms that this outbreak of the repressed unconscious may take is an impulse disorder such as kleptomania. In kleptomania the repressed unconscious is acting directly in the world, over the head of an ego that is relatively helpless to prevent it from running its course. Nor can the enactor of this drama usually understand what the unconscious wants. The unconscious is speaking in symbolic language, much as it does in dreams, only here it is speaking with action.

My kleptomaniacal midlifer had, through her previous development, formed an identity and a pattern of consciousness that occluded her awareness of what she wanted for herself. This severe attenuation of her capacity to wish directly for herself had occurred in order to develop the capacity to respond to the wishes of others, and it had reached such a degree of hyperextension that she no longer knew what her own wishes and preferences might be or even that she might be wishing for something. Her behavior was telling her, therefore, what she was unconscious of in the way of wishing.

Hermes, on the other hand, displays such an exceedingly different relation to impulse and wish that, if it is indeed he who is showing his face in kleptomania, he is doing so in a highly distorted form. Yet by our retaining the viewpoint that Hermes does indeed make an appearance within this disorder of the impulse to steal, it may be possible to understand how the unconscious might be attempting self-healing through this symptom.

Perhaps it is true of all the Greek gods and goddesses, but particularly so of Hermes, that the relation of consciousness to impulse is so utterly direct and immediate. This is dramatized on the very first day of Hermes' existence. Hungry for meat, he knows his wish and rustles Apollo's cattle. No time is needed to mull things over and wonder what he wants. He has direct access to his desire and knows what will satisfy it. More than that. For Hermes, wishing is intimately linked to acting. Consciousness of impulse leads directly to action. No Hamlet ("'sicklied o'er with the pale cast of thought'") in Hermes! And because of this close linkage among consciousness, impulse, and action, there is immediate and wholehearted effort: Hermes' whole being consciously enters the action.

The contrasts between this Hermetic pattern and the kleptomaniacal behavior of my analysand are worthy of some close consideration. Whereas Hermes immediately recognizes what he wants and takes the most direct way of getting it, namely, thieving, she could reach the object of her wish only indirectly, through acting out under the pressure of an unconsciously determined compulsion to steal it; then (perhaps) she could recognize what she was wanting through observing what she was thieving (cosmetics = Aphrodite, charm, female attractiveness, value). Because she could not wish for the object directly, she had to steal it to find out that she wanted it. Kleptomania was the (albeit obscure and indirect) means for contacting this repressed wish, and the distorted epiphany of Hermes as this compulsion to steal was the messenger and guide into that dark, neglected, and locked-away corner of her psyche where the healing, compensating impulse was hidden.

If these reflections on the psychological dynamics and meaning of kleptomania are accurate and can therefore be cashed out pragmatically in deepened understanding and changed behavior, it should happen that this compulsion to steal will be reduced in severity if the wish to which it leads is made conscious and accepted as a legitimate and health-restoring wish. And certainly this is the tactic and aim of therapeutic treatment. But accepting this wish as legitimate, and indeed as healthy, is precisely the most difficult thing for a kleptomaniacal patient to do. Because the relation to impulse and wish is disturbed in this person, the object to which desire would lead must be taken in an act that is doubly deceptive. Stealing it out of an unconsciously determined compulsion amounts to this sort of double-deception: first the 'others' are deceived, then it is oneself, who now has the object as though not having acquired it. While Hermes deceives only once, the kleptomaniac must deceive twice.

The wish and its object *cannot* be accepted as legitimate. They are taboo, stained by shadow, and therefore banished from conscious ownership. And the resultant disturbance in the relation to impulse and wish produces a reversal that furthers the aim of self-deception. Where with Hermes the sequence of events runs (a) consciousness of the impulse, appetite, or desire, and of its object, (b) action, (c) conscious sacrifice of the desired object (to the other gods), for the kleptomaniac the sequence is (a) unconscious sacrifice of the wish (through repression), (b) doubly-deceptive action, and (c) (rarely) consciousness of the wish. Yet, despite this duplicitous effort to lock out the repressed contents of the unconscious even while being forced to act on the unconscious wish, the ruse does not work, and the double-deceiver is tricked into owning the forbidden object anyway. This is the 'gift' of Hermes.

Whenever Hermes appears, even if it is in a disguised and distorted epiphany such as kleptomania, he induces contact with a remote, unconscious content; he is a messenger, the go-between, for an unconscious complex that is a combination of wishes, desires, impulses, thoughts, and images clustered around an archetypal core. But the ego, entrenched as it is in its habits and identifications, quite understandably resists this messenger, much like it has resisted the pressure of the complex itself in the past. So in also now resisting the compulsion, the ego's resistance must be doubled, and this creates a conscious state of intense anxiety, as described in the *Harvard Guide*: "The actions [of kleptomania] are accompanied by an inconspicuous but real neurotic alteration in character, with chronic anxiety beyond the immediate fear of being caught, guilt, fear of losing one's mind, shame, and, usually, inhibition of normal sexual responses" (p. 292). It is actually the ego's resistance to the pressure of the unconscious, specifically to what is being generated from the region of shadow, that makes Hermes appear in this shadowy form, kleptomania, in the first place. One way or another, however, the shadow returns at midlife, and the graves open and reveal their dead.

These reflections on the presence of the gods in our psychopathologies, and specifically on the epiphany of Hermes as kleptomania, serve several purposes here. They are a venture in archetypal psychopathology, an attempt to understand, by taking the action of archetypes into account, the psychological dynamics and meaning of pathological behavior. The suffering of the patients who bring these disorders of the soul into the analytic consulting room cannot be grasped without recognizing the archetypal dimension of the unconscious operative in the background.

These thoughts are also aimed at casting some light on how and why the repressed contents of the shadow return to consciousness at midlife, particularly during its liminality period. In a way, I am expanding on the point made in the last chapter that conscious retrieval of 'corpses' is essential to the task of moving into and through midlife liminality. But these are very different corpses from the ones needing burial discussed in the previous chapter. These are unfinished developmental possibilities rather than outworn structures of the conscious personality. When the unconscious erupts at midlife, what first comes most strongly to the fore are rejected pieces of personality that were left undeveloped and cast aside sometime in the past, for one reason or another, in the rapid movement forward of personal history. Life still clings strongly to them. And actually the seeds of the future lie in these neglected figures, which now return and call for restoration and attention.

As pointed out before, the entry into the experience of liminality at midlife occurs typically through the door of loss, defeat, mourning, and burial. Working through the psychological separation this experience entails leads to the possibility for psychological 'floating,' an attitude of unattachment essential to existence in liminality. 'Floating' requires, and then brings with it, a more direct relation to the impulses than is demanded, or even desirable, during more settled and stable eras of life. Now there is a direct, immediate connection to the wish, the desire, the impulse, and this is hinged directly to action, as is told of Hermes: on the first day of his existence, "craving for meat / he leaped from the fragrant dwelling and went forth scouting,/ pondering some bold wile in his mind. . ." (*Hymn*, 64–66). So, when we move Hermetically in liminality, consciousness registers desire immediately and moves into action, planning ways to satisfy it.

In psychology, and particularly in depth psychology and psychoanalysis, a traditional theme of discussion is 'acting out.' This is action undertaken by a person for reasons that are obscure and unconscious to him; here the relation between ego and impulse or wish is obfuscated by various defenses, such as denial, repression, or projection. The actions that are characteristic of persons suffering from an impulse disorder, like kleptomania, fall into this category: theirs are 'acting out' actions. Hermetic action, however, is entirely different. It is precisely *not* 'acting out' but rather conscious enactment. Here the relation between ego and impulse is clear and uncluttered by defenses, or even by rationalizations. What Hermes teaches, then—keeping in mind that we are trying to learn from him how to move within the midlife experience of liminality—is the lesson of enactment: conscious wish-fulfillment. It is because the ego enters into such close relation to the unconscious during liminality that it is now capable of this. It actually becomes, in part, Hermes-like.

To act toward fulfilling the wishes of the Self and to relate this directly to desire facilitate the compensatory action of the unconscious upon consciousness. The wish is a signal, a message from the unconscious, and its fulfillment is geared precisely to what a one-sided ego-consciousness needs for its completeness. Where is Hermes led by his wish for meat and by the thieving impulse? To Apollo's cattle and to Apollo, the polar counterpart to Hermes in the Olympian pantheon. And where is the kleptomaniacal analysand led—this woman who has devoted her previous years of adulthood to the Demetrian pattern of motherhood and the nurture of others and who has erased from her consciousness all flickers of personal desiring in favor of registering the desires of others—but to the cosmetic counter, an island in the province of Aphrodite? The epiphany of Hermes (in kleptomania) guides her to the archetype that, severely repressed in her past, is most needed for her own completeness as a woman in the present and the future. So it may be that, if you follow the thieving impulse far enough, you come upon the archetypal structure from which you need to have something.

Rafael Lopez-Pedraza suggests another closely related implication of Hermetic theft: "The image of this first theft, and one committed against Hermes' own brother Apollo, offers a certain speculative idea: psychological thieving is invariably done to someone who, for one reason or another, is close to us, akin: in the tale the theft takes place within the kinship of brotherhood. One has to be close enough to thieve psychologically, for one psyche to thieve from another" (p. 31). By following the impulse Hermetically, i.e., immediately and directly along the natural gradient of libido, one comes into a liminal situation where a relationship that has been tacit can be revealed and established as a conscious relationship. This path to relationship opens up precisely because the sacrosanct boundary between 'mine' and 'yours,' the key to intrapsychic as well as interpersonal 'distance,' has been overcome. Our crossing this borderline reveals the secret bond of affinity and kinship. Just as envy tells us what we have neglected in ourselves, so thievish impulses tell what we need, to whom we are already tacitly related in kinship, and what we need to integrate.

But it is essential to recognize that Hermes is not trapped by his theft, as he would be if now he assumed the position of Apollonic ownership and clung to this as a new identity. He avoids getting caught up in this kind of enantiodromic movement into the opposite and does *not* become Apollonic after he thieves Apollo's property. He stays liminal.

To thieve Hermetically means pursuing and taking what is desired and following the impulse to its conclusion in action, but then, paradoxically, letting go of the spoils that have been taken. Here is sacrifice. Not that the Hermetic thief suddenly suffers guilt and shamefacedly returns the spoils to their original owner. Hermes certainly does not do this, but he does not actually eat the meat he was earlier craving, either. He uses the spoils, rather, to create a relation to the other gods, by turning them into a sacrifice. In this way, Hermes retains his freedom to 'float' and does not fall into an identification with his new possessions. These are used to bring about relationship, not destroy it by creating a new system of 'yours' and 'mine,' 'I and not-I' distinctions. Similarly, as the *Hymn* shows, the aim of stealing Apollo's cattle is to create a connection between this new wild thing recently come into the world (the 'illegitimate child,' Hermes) and the established dominant complex (the 'legitimated owner,' Apollo). The exchange of gifts between Hermes and Apollo—Hermes' invention (the lyre) for Apollo's possession (the cattle)—represents a flow of libido between two archetypal structures, one newly emergent from the unconscious, the other established and dominant. Building this bridge between ego-consciousness and the unconscious is both the central psychological task of midlife and its greatest opportunity for individuation.

Chapter Five

The Lure to Soul-Mating
in Midlife Liminality

> Journeying is the best condition for loving. The
> gorges over which the "volatized one" passes
> like a ghost can be the abysses of unbelievable
> love affairs—Circe and Calypso islands. . . .
>   Kerényi

"Archetypes were, and still are, living psychic forces that demand
to be taken seriously, and they have a strange way of making sure of
their effects," Jung writes (1959a, §266), and in the previous
chapter I analyzed their workings in an episodic appearance of kleptomania at midlife. The general point of the chapter was that at midlife "the repressed"—in Jungian terminology, the "shadow"—
returns and needs to be dealt with in a new way, because the seeds of
psychological renewal and of possible future directions for life lie
hidden within it. These seeds may germinate into a vocation, and
they will certainly demand further, and often unpredictable, psychological development.

If the psychological contents that were once personified as gods
and 'powers' are not defunct but continue to appear today in our
psychopathologies, making these illnesses actually disguised signals
from unconscious soul figures, this should not be construed to mean
that their range of appearance is restricted to grossly pathological
forms. Dreams, spontaneous fantasies, visions, synchronistic events,
"complex reactions"—these psychological phenomena, which some

might consider minor pathologies, also herald the presence of archetypes. One of Jung's strokes of genius was to recognize that the
proximity of an archetype to consciousness can have a psychologically protective function: its presence is not always pathological even
though inevitably it disturbs consciousness. "Always they [i.e., the
archetypes] were bringers of protection and salvation," Jung adds to
the lines quoted above, and this observation forms the kernel of
thought around which the present chapter is organized.

I wish to consider the role of *Hermes as guardian* and relate this
to the experience of midlife liminality. The questions I wonder about
are these: What do you need to be most critically protected *from*
during midlife liminality? Then, how does the unconscious protect
you from the destruction to which it seems itself to be leading as
you pass through midlife liminality? And finally, what can be
learned from the stories about the mythic figure Hermes that will
shed light on how the unconscious guards you during midlife
liminality and on how it functions as a "bringer of protection and
salvation"?

It is certainly something of a paradox that we should look to
Hermes as a bringer of protection against the onslaughts of the unconscious at midlife since, as I pointed out in the last chapter, he
represents such a direct and spontaneous relation to impulse, and it
is precisely from this area that you would expect danger at midlife.
So the question naturally arises: if you become Hermetic during
midlife liminality and 'float' in more-or-less (or at least more-than-
usual) immediate contact with your impulses and emergent unconscious contents, what is to prevent you from running amuck with
impulsivity, or from indulging what turn out to be deeply regressive
urges, or from succumbing to gross pleasure-seeking and to the
"id" with its proclivity to perversion and its destructive potential?

This suspicious view of human nature and of where impulses will
lead if you give them free rein cannot be discounted as merely an

outmoded legacy of Judeo-Christian religion and of its conditioning to a felt sense of original sin. The great modernist Freud offers a wholly secularized version of this distrustful evaluation of the human condition, and Jung, too, with his doctrines of the shadow and a dark side of the Self, certainly does not overlook or reject this view of reality. The perception of a deeply ingrained human potential for regression and self-destructive behavior can be found, too, in myth, religion, and story all over the world, and so it most likely reflects archetypal structures and represents a universally valid truth about mankind.

What may be parochial and unduly pessimistic, however, is the suspicion that nature cannot be trusted to treat nature. When a split is created between nature and culture, and culture is seen as mankind's only protection from destruction, then ego-consciousness becomes our only hope, and we fearfully conclude that without external cultural and legal prohibitions and enforcements individual human beings and the human race as a whole will degenerate and sink irretrievably into regressive attitudes and behavior. While this opinion certainly overestimates the potential of ego-consciousness for remedying the human predicament, it also fails to recognize that the taboo against regression is itself archetypal and that there actually exists, therefore, an effective protective mechanism within human nature itself against this danger. So another way of stating the question for this chapter is: How does nature protect you against nature during midlife liminality?

Recall that a person's sense of direction forward is beclouded and obscured during liminality; life's pathways to the future appear to be unmarked and even uncharted, and the future itself seems unimaginable in every conceivable direction. Behind is the period of destructuring and separation: of general breakdown in persona and identity, in consciously held and affirmed value priorities, in self-images, dreams for the future, and ideals. These have been put away, and the release of the soul that was housed in them opens the gate into an era of psychological 'floating.' Now the way is unfamiliar and ambiguous: collective values, the ideals of youth, old habits do not guide anymore, and there is anxious uncertainty about which direction to take. A person seems to stand perpetually at some inner crossroads, confused and torn. The psychological functions and the attitude that have been guides and counselors in the past are faded voices, and when consulted they do not seem able to persuade very convincingly anymore. And then it happens, too, that the craving for a soul-mate—how else can I say it?—which had been deflected in the past, or diverted to other ends, or perhaps had never even been aroused with much intensity before, invades consciousness and massages into it this longing for, and vision of, complete psychological intimacy. And so the question of how to relate to *this* wish, to *this* vision, becomes acute during midlife liminality. Can we look to Hermes, then, to this god of wanderers and of souls in passage, for some assistance during this phase of the soul's passage through midlife liminality?

I want to reflect on this set of psychological circumstances during midlife liminality, and on the protection Hermes offers in it, by looking at the Circe episode in the *Odyssey*, taking this episode as classically emblematic of this phase of the midlife transition. This episode represents, to use Jung's terminology, a man's midlife encounter with the anima. And it is during this fateful meeting, itself a critical pivot point for the journey as a whole, that Hermes makes one of his most winsome appearances, proving himself to be the protector of that archetypal wanderer, Odysseus, who represents the soul's long journey and passage through liminality. In this episode, Circe, a seductress and enchantress, exercises power over weary and unwary men by drawing them to her with a sweet voice and then plying them with wine and drugs and finally turning them into swine by the magic of her wand. Obviously, her island represents a potential danger on the passage through midlife liminality.

The encounter with Circe takes place in the tenth Book of the *Odyssey*. This Book opens with high hopes for a speedy return to Ithaka: Aiolos, the king of a floating island and a favorite of the gods, gives Odysseus a bag ''made of the skin taken off a nine-year / ox, stuffed full inside with the courses of all the blowing / winds . . . tied fast with a silver / string, so there should be no wrong breath of wind, not even / a little'' and sets ''the West Wind free to blow me and carry / the ships and the men aboard them on their way'' toward home (10: 19–26). And this scheme works wonderfully well, bringing the ships into sight of the long-sought homeland. But then Odysseus, confident that he has returned home, unaccountably has to take a nap. When he awakes, he finds to his astonishment and horror that his men have stupidly untied the bag and freed the chaotic winds, which have blown them all the way back to where they began, to the island of King Aiolos.

This setback raises a topic that deserves consideration in these reflections on the vicissitudes of the soul during midlife liminality: just as the drifting and wandering seem to be drawing to an end and some resolution comes into sight, there is a critical loss of consciousness, and it's back to square one all over again. This is as commonplace as it is distressing: in this phase of the midlife transition there is much repetition of the same patterns, recycling, blowing back and forth, covering the same ground all over again. Consciousness does not seem able to hold 'lessons' and to learn from experience. And so all movement *looks* circular. But it should be remembered that Hermes, who favors retrograde movement (cf. Lopez-Pedraza, pp. 31–32), may create regressions that are disguised as mere repetitions, each one actually deepening the experience of liminality and leading to a more profound experience of the depths of psychic existence. These are regressions in the service of the Self: they lead consciousness downward to its sources in the unconscious.

But I move on, because the episode to which this return leads Odysseus and his companions is what is of interest now. When the devastated wayfarers arrive back at the island of Aiolos, the king rejects them, and so they launch their ships once again and proceed on their own. Most of the crew is lost when the giant Laistrygones attacks their ships with huge boulders, and the survivors arrive on the shores of Circe's island heartsick and exhausted: "There we disembarked, and for two days and two nights / We lay there, for sorrow and weariness eating our hearts out" (10: 142–43).

This state of depletion and exhaustion is a predictable moment within the experience of midlife liminality and, in the *Odyssey*, a preliminary for the appearance of Hermes. Not knowing where they are or what they will find on this strange island, Odysseus addresses his comrades: "'Hear my words, my companions, in spite of your heart's sufferings. / Dear friends . . . we do not know where the darkness is nor the sunrise, / nor where the Sun who shines upon people rises, nor where / he sets . . . let us hasten our minds and think, whether there is / any course left open to us'" (10: 189–93).

Where, and what, is the land to which these men have come? Clearly it is not within the boundaries of the 'normal' world. Its landscape is mythic, and its owner is a faded goddess: Circe. Kerényi comments on the suggestiveness of these lines in the *Odyssey* and speculates on the locations of Circe's island:

> There was a special reason, rooted in the mythological perception of landscape forms, why the Greeks believed they recognized the island of Circe . . . off the west coast of Italy, at what is today Monte Circei. This place is connected to the mainland by a swampy path—called, before their draining, the Pontic swamps; earlier it was separated from the mainland by the same swamp and was thus an island wilderness. In this place, surrounded by sea and swamp, whose headlands were still covered with forest when I visited the place, and whose landscape in the moonlight I experienced as almost enchantingly bewitched, that great archaic Goddess, whose silhouette we discover around Circe if we read the tenth book of the *Odyssey* carefully, could well be at home. (1979, pp. 6–7)

Kerényi sees Circe as a faded version of "that great archaic God-dess," a combination of Aphrodite and the "Mistress of Wild Animals," who is also known as the Near-Eastern Great Goddess. So it is into this realm of the archetypal feminine that Odysseus comes at this crucial point in his liminal odyssey, and he must now deal with the Goddess.

If we regard the Circe episode as we would the *dream* of a man passing through midlife liminality, we may avoid the hazard of get-ting stuck at the level of a host of superficial parallels to conscious experience. We want to engage a more trenchant hermeneutic that will expose the dynamics of the personal and collective unconscious and thereby uncover the "common core of unconscious meaning," the archetypal dimension, beneath these parallel lines. The episode, it must be said, lends itself naturally to this level of interpretation because of the magical transformations that take place in Circe's do-main. Transformations in form, such as these, are as familiar in dreams as they are bizarre to normal waking consciousness and common sense. So the text itself begs interpreting at the level of un-conscious process. Finally, this type of interpretation helps to steer clear of grossly moralistic observations and reflections, which in-evitably end up obscuring the more subtle psychological meanings of events such as this one. So I put the questions this way: What does the Circe episode say about the state of the psyche during midlife liminality? And, how does Hermes function as a protector, and what does his assistance mean psychologically, in this critical testing period of the midlife transition?

A standard Jungian opening for interpreting dreams (cf. 1969, §561) looks to the dream's *setting* for the first clue to the un-conscious core of meaning that it represents. According to Kerényi's scholarship, the text places the Circe episode in the realm of "that great archaic Goddess," the Near-Eastern Mother- and Love-Goddess, and so this story forms one more link in that much larger and quite pervasive "dream series" in the *Odyssey*, Odysseus's encounters with the archetypal feminine. But this moment in Odysseus's journey, when he meets up and deals with Circe, is special. Its symbolism shows it to be the equivalent to what Jung often refers to as a return to the mother (cf. for example 1970a, §351 ff.), a point in the individuation process, typically occurring at midlife, when themes of early childhood, of symbiotic union with the mother, and of a heightened need for nurturing and psychological intimacy are constellated, all of which reflect the intrapsychic need for ego-consciousness to reestablish contact with its source, the (maternal) unconscious. What can be mistaken as a merely regressive pull toward orality and fusion with the mother (or with a mother symbol, a carrier of this projection) actually indicates the need to work out a new kind of relationship with the unconscious, which appears in the form of a contrasexual figure (symbolically or in projection), the anima in a man, the animus in a woman. The Circe episode portrays the dangers inherent in this descent into the unconscious and also the rewards and renewal that can come from a successful negotiation of these troubled waters. But success in this venture, as the story indicates, depends on the timely protection and assistance of another figure of the unconscious, Hermes.

As the story-line goes, the survivors spend two days resting on the shores of Circe's island before beginning to explore it. Odysseus stays on ship while the others go inland, where they soon come upon Circe's palace and hear her "singing in a sweet voice" as she goes up and down a loom weaving a "delicate and lovely and glorious" design (221–22). Not suspecting the least danger, the starving men accept Circe's generous hospitality—"a potion, with barley and cheese and pale honey added to Pramnian wine" (234–35)—unaware of the "malignant drugs" laced into the mixture that will make them "forgetful of their own country" (236). Having satisfied their appetites and attended to their hunger, Circe suddenly strikes them with her wand, transforms them into pigs, and drives them into her pig pens. So the companions, whose minds remain unaltered, now inhabit bodies of pigs. Only one, a suspicious fellow named Eurylochos, who waited outside the palace because he suspected treachery, escapes this transformation and hurries to inform Odysseus of the tragedy. Odysseus cannot be convinced to sail away immediately and to abandon his comrades but instead sets out to find them in hopes of rescuing them from their fallen porcine condition. On the way to Circe's palace, Odysseus meets Hermes "in the likeness of a young man / with beard new grown, which is the most graceful time of young manhood" (278–79), and this conversation ensues:

"Where are you going, unhappy man, all alone, through the
    hilltops,
ignorant of the land-lay, and your friends are here in Circe's
place, in the shape of pigs and holed up in the close pig pens.
Do you come here meaning to set them free? I do not think
you will get back yourself, but must stay here with the others.
But see, I will find you a way out of your troubles, and save you.
Here, this is a good medicine, take it, and go into Circe's
house; it will give you power against the day of trouble.
And I will tell you all the malevolent guiles of Circe.
She will make you a potion, and put drugs in the food, but she
    will not
even so be able to enchant you, for this good medicine
which I give you now will prevent her. I will tell you the details
of what to do. As soon as Circe with her long wand strikes you,
then drawing from beside your thigh your sharp sword, rush
forward against Circe, as if you were raging to kill her,
and she will be afraid, and invite you to go to bed with her.
Do not then resist and refuse the bed of the goddess,
for she will set free your companions, and care for you also;

but bid her swear the great oath of the blessed gods, that she
has no other evil hurt that she is devising against you,
so she will not make you weak and unmanned, once you are
  naked.''
  'So spoke Argeiphontes, and he gave me [Odysseus] the
    medicine,
which he picked out of the ground, and he explained the nature
of it to me. It was black at the root, but with a milky
flower. The gods call it moly. It is hard for mortal
men to dig up, but the gods have power to do all things.'

(281–306)

By following these instructions of Hermes, Odysseus does indeed
establish a fruitful relationship with Circe and gets his men released
from their enchantment. All spend a year on her island recovering
their strength and morale, and at the end of it, feeling restless to be
on their way home, they receive instructions from the goddess for
the next step of their voyage: they must go to Hades and there inter-
view the blind seer, Teiresias, who will ''tell you the way to go, the
stages of your journey'' (539). Upon hearing this horrendous news,
the men ''sat on the ground and lamented and tore their hair
out, / but there came no advantage to them for all their sorrowing''
(567–68).

The Circe episode portrays a classic picture of midlife individuation: confrontation with the anima (Circe), leading to a consciously
worked-out relationship with this figure, followed by a further descent into liminality (Hades) and a meeting with the figure of a wise
old man (Teiresias). For the moment, however, my reflections bear
on Circe, on the kind of threat she represents and on the kind of
help Hermes offers to turn this threat into a key opportunity for
further individuation.

The ''midlife crisis'' is the subject of much defensive humor
because it is frightening, often being marked by a massive eruption

of what seems to be regression-driven libido. The acutely intense emotionality, the touchy moodiness, the rash impulsiveness—states of mind and feeling and patterns of behavior that are usually more associated with adolescents and small children than with their parents—disrupt the functioning of 'normal' adult ego-consciousness. Adults are not expected to act and feel like this. During midlife liminality, especially, such seemingly infantile and adolescent emotional patterns may take hold and seem even more compulsive and irrational then they were in childhood. "Oh, the midlife crisis" is the ironic, and defensively dismissive, remark made about middle-aged business tycoons who drive sports cars and leave wives to run off with leggy young secretaries, or about successful and established physicians who scandalize themselves by taking up with nurses not much older than their daughters, or about suburban housewives and mothers who are compelled to rush into Dionysian love affairs with tai chi instructors and bus drivers. All of this is socially disruptive, seemingly irrational, and quite horrifying because it could happen to *you*!

Jung formulated his theory of the anima and animus, the archetypal structures behind this invasion of libido, during his own period of midlife liminality, in the years of "Confrontation with the Unconscious," 1912 to 1918, between the ages of thirty-seven and forty-three (cf. *MDR*, pp. 170–99). His views on these archetypal *daimons* and on their overwhelming power and influence over consciousness were not the outgrowth of observing adolescents or the product of objective academic research. They were deeply rooted in his own intense anima experiences and in similar experiences of the adults with whom he was working analytically at the time. The power of the anima and animus to lure and to attract and to fascinate, whether experienced in the charged landscape of big dreams or in obsessive fantasies of adventure and romance or in relationship with persons who embody these unconscious figures and carry their projected images, is generated by the urgent impulse to unite a pair of essential psychological opposites. The potency of this vision of union lies in its promising the deepest imaginable psychological healing. But this intense urgency to unite with the person who embodies the perfect soul-mate carries in it, as well, the power to create and sustain a breathtaking degree of illusion and self-deception. This gives it the power to work magic on the perceptions of ego-consciousness. The anima is Maya, spinner of fantasy and illusion (cf. Jung 1959b, §20 ff.), and in her hand she holds the wand of Circe.

In his autobiography, Jung described an instance of attempted anima seduction that clued him into how this figure operates and also into how to deal with such appearances of unconscious wishfulness and thinking. Its parallels to the Circe episode are striking. Jung writes (1961, pp. 185–86) that at one point during his "confrontation with the unconscious" he fell into grave doubt about the scientific value of his work, and the thought occurred to him that what he was doing was not science but "art." He was producing fascinating drawings and paintings (and, from his paintings, it does seem that he was actually artistically talented), and since they weren't science, this inner voice said, they must be art! He was not a medical doctor or a scientist but an artist! When this rather glamorous thought passed through his head, he listened to it, but objectively, as a scientist attends to a curious phenomenon. He recognized it as the internalized seductive "voice" of a female patient of his, "a talented psychopath" (p. 185). (Here we can recognize the wily Circe at work, casting her spell of enchantment and beclouding a person's sense of identity, which is vague during liminality anyway.) Jung did not, however, dismiss this thought out of hand but dealt with it experimentally, by allowing it, and the figure behind it, to speak freely, even giving his vocal cords over to her and letting her have her full say. Then he could evaluate the message: from its content and tone, he concluded that it was an anima-lure away from his already settled vocation, a kind of siren song that would lead him to Paris and then leave him high and dry in a bohemian garret, like Odysseus's comrades stuck in a foreign land in an alien life-form.

Jung's suspiciousness of the anima figure and of her potential for enchantment has parallels in the Circe tale, first in the figure of the companion Eurylochos and then in Hermes' advice to Odysseus. A similar healthy suspiciousness of the intentions of alluring persons is commonly found among men and women at midlife. Where will they lead you if you give in to your impulses and longings and follow them? Can you trust them, or will they abandon you at a critical moment of vulnerability? Will they use you and cast you aside? Will you give up what you have worked for to discover one day that you have made a fool of yourself? Doubtful thoughts such as these crowd into consciousness and into dreams during midlife liminality, and well they should. This is healthy paranoia and helps a person avoid getting stuck at this stage of the journey.

This spontaneous outburst of suspicious thinking depends as much on the workings of the unconscious as seductive anima-thinking does, and it is one aspect of nature's protection against nature. It prevents naive regression to infantile levels of emotional development: human consciousness ensnared in the body of a pig, an image for the ego's regression to the stage of oral gratification and infantile dependency on a nurturing mother, while the more highly developed levels of cognition remain intact and functional. Here the rational mind can know, analyze, and understand a state of affairs, but the appetites, urges, hungers, dependencies, and other affective states remain in charge of emotional reaction and of actual behavior.

This threat of regressive degeneration into a pig-existence, with the ego locked helplessly in bondage to somatic and instinctual processes and cravings and to their literal gratification, confronts us as a critical, and rightly feared, midlife transformation. With the ideals and dreams of youth dead and buried, what is there to life but greedy self-gratification? Without a healthy sense of suspiciousness and a method for dealing with this crisis of the spirit, a possibility does exist of getting stuck here. 'Being stuck' represents a state of helpless attachment to the view that this is literally all there is to life. (Circe's drugs cause the companions to forget their homeland.) As a psychological attitude, it is radically reductive to the concretely infantile substratum of animal existence. What else is there to human life and spirit but raw physicality, its promptings, and anxiety about its demise? This helplessness is backed by an odd sort of innocence about what is going on, as though it were all quite natural (given you are not all hung up in moral restraints and collective taboos!) to pursue literal wealth and power with unrestrained greed, to gain thirty pounds and to keep on getting fatter at midlife, to rely on the bottle in the liquor cabinet and the fourth drink before dinner to get through the evening, or to indulge in one casual sexual encounter after another without much emotional reward for all the effort. A person can become so entangled in these patterns of gratification and the cynicism that goes with them that ego-consciousness is rendered too feeble to do anything about the situation. All that is left for the rational mind to do is calculate costs and benefits. This is middle-aged logos!

We can read Baudelaire's lines—

> Stupidity, delusion, selfishness and lust
> torment our bodies and possess our minds. . . .
>
> the Devil's hand directs our every move—
> the things we loathed become the things we love;
> day by day we drop through stinking shades
> quite undeterred on our descent to Hell.
>
> Like a poor profligate who sucks and bites
> the withered breast of some well-seasoned trull,
> we snatch in passing at clandestine joys
> and squeeze the oldest orange harder yet.

(P. 5)

—as a gloss on this picture from the *Odyssey*:

> When she had given them this and they had drunk it down, next
>   thing
> she struck them with her wand and drove them into her pig pens,
> and they took on the look of pigs, with the heads and voices
> and bristles of pigs, but the minds within them stayed as they had
>   been
> before. So crying they went in, and before them Circe
> threw down acorns for them to eat, and ilex and cornel
> buds, such food as pigs who sleep on the ground always feed on.
>
>   (10: 237–43)

So the suspiciousness of this anima trap represents one side of Hermes' guardianship at this dangerous moment during the journey through midlife liminality. But more than that, the 'idea' for how to deal creatively, and not only defensively, with the anima-enchantress comes to Odysseus through the epiphany of Hermes. Hermes advises Odysseus both on how to avoid the danger of being drawn into a pig-existence and on how to use this encounter with the goddess to advantage.

In our 'dream,' then, Hermes appears not only as a reflection of Odysseus's own timely suspiciousness but as a *god* who brings protection through giving him something he could not have gotten for himself. So what do the gifts of Hermes to Odysseus represent, taken as timely gifts from the unconscious at the moment of a man's midlife transition when the anima must be dealt with?

First, the moly. Scholars are divided on what kind of herb this was, although there does seem to be some agreement that it had to do with witchcraft. My preference is to follow the thinking of the scholars and botanists who identify moly as a type of Mediterranean garlic (*Allium victorialis*) that was credited with magical properties (Rahner, p. 186); this view links up with the overall theme of this chapter, which is the encounter with the enchanting power and the regressive pull of the anima at midlife.

Garlic was generally associated in ancient times with witches and witchcraft, or with counter-witchcraft, and "was placed at cross-roads for Hecate and also carried by travelers to protect them from her" (Funk and Wagnalls, p. 441). Hermes' gift of moly, therefore, brings him into association with Hecate, the Greek goddess of witches and witchcraft and of black magic. Their association through the moly-garlic root is reinforced by the further similarity that the shrines of both deities were located at crossroads. This affinity between Hermes and Hecate points toward the idea that what Hermes is giving Odysseus to counteract the enchantment and the bewitching power of Circe is a bit of witchcraft. A successful encounter with the enchantment of the anima/goddess figure during midlife liminality certainly does require some conscious likeness to her, so that when she is met she is not a total stranger, alien and foreign and therefore unknown in her ways; rather she is met as a familiar. Odysseus needs something of an enchantress-witch-anima-consciousness in order to meet and not be taken in by Circe or fall victim to her powers. Hermes helps Odysseus gain this kind of symmetry with Circe. And he can do this precisely because he knows so well the impulses and hungers on which Circe's transformational power rests.

If Hermes represents what might be termed an archetype of suspicion, or healthy paranoia, which is related to his identity as a trickster (the trickster being always on guard against tricks), he also represents, as we saw earlier, a direct relation to the impulses. And it is precisely because he does have such a clear relation to wish and impulse that he can provide the standpoint by which entrapment in the regressive pull of the anima can be consciously resisted. As it takes a thief to catch a thief, so it takes a wizard and a magician to catch an enchantress at her tricks and to avoid her traps.

Recall Jung's facing the anima's seductive temptation to declare his work art and himself an artist. To see through and to resist this enchanting and seductive thought, he had to recognize the source of the impulse (the face behind the voice). The consciousness Hermes brings is consciousness of the impulse and of its source (the face of the anima-enchantress), and this creates protection against the unconscious behavior it can induce if one is simply entranced by it. Unconscious, it has more power to bewitch, because it can induce acting out, which is action based on unconsciously motivated wishes and desires.

So, moly in your pocket when you meet up with the anima at midlife represents that bit of integrated Hermes-consciousness that tells you the nature of the impulse and its source and thereby puts you in a position to stand up against it.

But resistance is not the last word for dealing with the anima at midlife—she *is*, after all, the soul-mate—and Hermes' advice to Odysseus goes much further than providing him with a strategy for resisting Circe's wiles, although this does come first and it is essential. Because Hermes knows Circe so well, he being himself a magician and an enchanter (''he mazes the eyes of those mortals / whose eyes he would maze, or wakes again the sleepers,'' as it is written in the Twenty-Fourth Book of the *Odyssey*: 3–4), he can offer Odysseus advice both on resistance, thereby protecting him in that initial but limited sense, and also on how to turn this inevitable encounter with the bewitching anima to use for his further journeying.

It seems necessary to go *through* an encounter with the anima at midlife if the individuation journey is to continue and if the midlife transition is to move from liminality into the next stage of integrating the personality around a new core. To shy away, to repress, to run from the island and declare it hostile and unsafe territory (à la Eurylochos, the inveterate skeptic and cynic) is to abort the process. And this leads to the same degree of stalemate in life as succumbing to the enchantment of Circe. It creates an aborted midlife transition that Jung called the regressive restoration of the persona (1966,

§254-59), a real enough danger and a not infrequent outcome of the "midlife crisis." Eurylochos represents this tendency to retreat from the challenge of encountering the unconscious deeply at midlife and coming to terms with it, and had Odysseus followed the panicky advice of this companion he would have abandoned his other companions to an eternal pig-existence and would himself have failed to deal with a central task of individuation at midlife.

As Lopez-Pedraza reiterates more than once in his book on Hermes, this god characteristically acts to put and to keep things in movement. In this instance of advising Odysseus, he does so by teaching him how to relate to Circe and how to understand the kind of help she can give him for continuing the journey later. So if Odysseus meets Circe in the correct fashion, she will further rather than block or hinder the passage forward:

> "As soon as Circe with her long wand strikes you,
> then drawing from beside your thigh your sharp sword, rush
> forward against Circe, as if you were raging to kill her,
> and she will be afraid, and invite you to go to bed with her.
> Do not then resist and refuse the bed of the goddess,
> for so she will set free your companions, and care for you also. . . ."
>
> (10: 293-98)

In this subtle interplay between resistance and submission, a relationship is worked out that frees the companions from their pig-existence and provides care and nurture for Odysseus as well.

An intriguing, if perhaps not altogether just, contrast to this type of Hermetic subtlety for dealing with the power of the feminine exists in the Biblical story of Joseph and Potiphar's Wife (Genesis 39): the account of a young man's virtuous resistance to a powerful, seductive woman, of his flight from her blandishments, and of his subsequent unjust imprisonment and exoneration. While the youthful Joseph moves in the archetypal pattern, so characteristic of

Biblical heroes, of innocence, victimization, and ultimate vindication, the middle-aged veteran of the Trojan war, wily Odysseus, does not. And, anyway, in the world of the *Odyssey* the intervention of Hermes precludes this kind of innocence and naivete and therefore both demands and provides a different strategy for dealing with the feminine, one in which the *goddess* is made to commit *herself* to the Hermetic wanderer's journey. But first Odysseus must get her to swear the "great oath." Hermes' final words of advice to him spell out the possible danger:

> "... bid her swear the great oath of the blessed gods, that she
> has no other evil hurt that she is devising against you,
> so she will not make you weak and unmanned, once you are naked."
>
> (299–301)

During midlife liminality, the seductiveness of the anima can be especially dangerous, her song fatefully attractive, and her promises unspeakably alluring; and it is important to resist falling naively into the hands of the Power. But, beyond that, there exists a chance now, as perhaps not before, to create—with Hermes' help!—a relationship of mutual equality and trust with this enchanter of the unconscious. So it is told in the *Odyssey* that, after Odysseus took his initial stand against Circe, threatened her, and resisted her overtures to eat and to drink, she invited him to enjoy the intimacy of her bed:

> "Come then, put away your sword in its sheath, and let us
> two go up into my bed so that, lying together
> in the bed of love, we may then have faith and trust in each other."
>
> (333–35)

And Odysseus accepts: "... after she had sworn me the oath, and made an end of it / I mounted the surpassingly beautiful bed of Circe" (346–47). Kerényi's commentary on this scene—on the need to have Circe swear the oath, on her surprising willingness to do so, and on its meaning—while characteristically cryptic is suggestive:

> Here there is no longer any talk about reconciliation but rather about faith and trust, about uttermost submission in undisguised self-surrender (this is the meaning of the simple Greek expression for trust). . . .It is part of Circe's hiddenness that she can also be "false," not through holding back but through allowing herself to exceed the human scale of the openly confiding Odysseus and thus to destroy him as a man. For this reason she must first swear the great oath. She does this because the circles of her magical power have been broken through and she has only herself left. (*Goddesses*, p. 19)

By following Hermes, then, Odysseus has broken through the magical power of the anima and has managed to get her to reduce herself to human magnitude and to commit herself to the human dimension. This is approximately equivalent psychologically to Job's effect on Yahweh as Jung discusses this in *Answer to Job*: through taking a firm stand against an archetypal Power, a person can bring it into relationship with human consciousness. So Odysseus is able to create a helpful relationship with Circe, a form of the Great Goddess, who represents in turn a major section of the collective unconscious. What is the help she gives him?

There is a surprise in the lines that describe the conclusion of the companions' immersion in pig-existence:

> . . . and Circe walked on through the palace,
> holding her wand in her hand, and opened the doors of the pigsty,
> and drove them out. They looked like nine-year-old porkers. They
>   stood
> ranged and facing her, and she, making her way through their
> ranks, anointed each of them with some other medicine,
> and the bristles, grown upon them by the evil medicine Circe
> had bestowed upon them before, now fell away from them,

and they turned back once more into men, younger than they had
    been
and taller for the eye to behold and handsomer by far.

(388–96)

It seems to me worthy of more note than scholars appear to have
given it that the companions' brief encounter with pig-existence had
a renewing, vitalizing effect on them: they are taller now, younger,
"handsomer by far" (as the text puts it) when they come out of
their enchanted state than they were going into it.

What has transpired is renewal. The symbolism of the renewal of
a worn-out and depleted psychological dominant through regression
into the "Mother's womb" and its subsequent transformation
there is paralleled in alchemy, where the Old King reenters the
mother, dissolves in her womb, and is later reborn as a revitalized
and youthful figure (cf. Jung, *CW* 14, §356 ff.). Odysseus's depleted
companions, who have undergone an immersion in the unconscious
and have been subjected to a prolonged and involuntary submission
to the anima—i.e., pig-existence: symbiotic union with depressive
moods, feelings of helplessness in the face of physical urges and cravings, somatizations symbolic of psychological conflict—have returned to their human identity with renewed energy and vigor.

The danger of becoming stuck in this regressed state has been sur-
mounted through the protective help of Hermes, himself an archetypal factor of the unconscious that helps a person's ego to split
away from the part of the psyche that is undergoing disintegrative
transformation and to 'float' through this liminal period. But more
than the ability for passively floating, the 'Hermes factor' gives you
the kind of subtle balance that provides what could loosely be called
a 'method' for standing up to the unconscious and its lure toward
regressive symbiosis with the anima: a combination of attitudes and
actions toward it that includes suspicion of it, active resistance

against it, and submission to it. The result of this Hermetic foot-work is an emerging trustworthy relationship to the unconscious. As a consequence of Odysseus's Hermes-inspired actions toward Circe, the enchantress is provoked into saying to the companions (and meaning it):

> "... But come now, eat your food and drink your wine, until
> you gather back again into your chests that kind of spirit
> you had in you when first you left the land of your fathers
> on rugged Ithaka. Now you are all dried out, dispirited
> from the constant thought of your hard wandering, nor is there any
> spirit in your festivity, because of so much suffering."
>
> (460–65)

Circe becomes, miraculously, a healer of spirit through the very means by which earlier she represented the threat of falling into a pig-existence: eating and drinking.

This complex and subtle interaction between a Hermes-inspired consciousness and the anima's promises of gratification represents a solution to the problem, posed at the beginning of this chapter, of how a person's ego, caught up in the fluidity of midlife liminality, can straightforwardly encounter the impulses and wishes that are be-ing concurrently constellated by unconscious forces and not be per-manently drawn under by them. How does nature protect us against nature? I asked, and I have responded that it does so by introducing an archetype, Hermes, which facilitates movement through this period and helps us avoid getting stuck in it. Without Hermes, Rafael Lopez-Pedraza has said, there are no transitions, only endless repetitions, a psychopathology without a god.*

But I have saved one piece of my response to this question for last. It is self-evidently essential for the kind of outcome represented by the conclusion of the Circe episode that consciousness know

*Personal communication, 1982.

what is being encountered. It is a gift of Hermes to Odysseus, and one of his most important, that he tells this hero of liminality who Circe is, that she is a *goddess* (297). This is Hermetic 'interpretation': it tells Odysseus what he is confronting. This is a type of hermeneutic that does not 'uncover' or 'reduce' or 'connect' or 'translate.' It *recognizes* and *sees*. It is vision. At midlife, in the encounter with the anima, you are dealing with a goddess!

This sense that there is a 'goddess' behind the urge and wish, or within the symptom, is essential for transforming the anima into a trustworthy friend and helper. She must be *seen*. I quote Jung's paper, ''The Psychology of the Child Archetype,'' once again: ''. . . every interpretation that comes anywhere near the hidden sense [of the symptom, the impulse, the fantasy, etc.] has always, right from the beginning, laid claim not only to absolute truth and validity but to instant reverence and religious devotion'' (1959a, §266). To face the anima is to face a goddess, and she must be recognized as such, approached correctly, and honored for what she is. This visionary insight, a gift of Hermes, into the issues at midlife illuminates that active and conscious encounter with the unconscious—confronted now in its true archetypal magnitude as a 'goddess'—as an essentially religious struggle.

Chapter Six

Through the Region of Hades
A Steep Descent in Midlife's Liminality

> . . . and the sun set, and all the journeying-ways
> were darkened.
>
> *Odyssey* 11: 12

Is there a key experience and, correspondingly, a set of key psychological tasks within the midlife transition that distinguish it from other transitional periods of life and give it its specific meaning?

Certainly, the experience of separating from an outmoded identity and the requirement of acknowledging the loss of this past self, grieving it, and putting it away are crucial. But this step, which is essentially one of separation from an earlier persona, is common to other transitional periods as well. Also common to all transitional periods is the experience of liminality and, during it, the task of confronting repressed elements within the personality as they return to consciousness in what are often pathological or regressive forms. More specific to the midlife transition is the encounter and the deliberate negotiation with the unconscious as a contrasexual opposite, as anima or animus. This experience, and especially the quality and meaning of this struggle, is quite distinctive of the midlife transition and is certainly critical to its outcome.

But the pivotal experience of the psychological change that unfolds at midlife, and the element that most unmistakably declares its uniqueness and brings it to its deepest meaning, is the lucid realization of death as life's personal, fated conclusion. The chilling awareness of this fact grips a person's consciousness at midlife as it has not gripped it before, and the sense of an absolute limit to personal extension in time spreads into every corner of consciousness and affects everything it touches. While this realization is not by itself the ultimate goal of the soul's transmutations during midlife, it is a critical catalyst in the chemistry of reaching that goal and one that leaves traces of itself indissolubly bound into the final product of the transformational process. The gold comes through the rust, the alchemists said (cf. Jung, 1953, §206–08), and this sense at midlife of death as an inescapable fate, waiting there implacably at the end of life's chronicity, *is* the rust.

It could be said with at least metaphoric truth that death itself actually occurs at midlife, as a person's identity and conscious attitudes go through profound internal transformations and become reorganized around a new core of psychological contents and meanings. At deeper and more unconscious levels, the archetypal dominants underlying the pattern of conscious self-organization and identity are changing: an old person is passing away. And until the pit of death is entered, the process of internal transformation cannot move to its conclusion, for at midlife, too, a new person is being born.

The phase of the midlife transition when this pit is entered and when the process of dissolving old psychological structures and reforming them around a new psychological core takes place is the liminal period. At the crux of midlife liminality is the experience that is imaged, dreamt, and felt as existing in a land of the dead: the end of the line, a city of ghosts, rooms without exit, senseless chronicity and repetition, despair. The movement into this psychological geography I call, following the journey of Odysseus, the descent to Hades: a place of the dead where there exist only pure naked souls. But it is within this descent into the dregs of liminal existence that there occurs an opportunity for consulting the Self that is not possible elsewhere. Here the Self does not have the puffed-up face of unlimited Potential, as it may have had in former years. In this consultation with the Self, now an image of long-lived wisdom and foundational truth, clues begin to appear for what will become a person's sense of core and for the life tasks that remain to be carried out. This is the gold.

So, in this chapter I am reflecting on what in the social sciences literature and in the popular press is generally and somewhat loosely referred to as "midlife death anxiety." But in using what Jung called the method of amplification to reflect upon the psyche's actions here, I am using an interpretive method very different from what is generally employed to investigate this phenomenon. The amplification method interprets psychological phenomena by starting from contemporary personal experience and moving to a larger, archetypal, and mythic perspective and then coming back again. This is the hermeneutic circle. Like any method of interpretation or research, this one can be misused and forced to absurdity and triviality. Since I would obviously hope to avoid doing this myself, I will pause here before directly pursuing the main theme of this chapter and make a sort of Hermetic sidewise movement toward it by first looking somewhat more carefully at this methodology and by considering what we are doing when we say, or think, that midlife involves a *nykia*, a "descent to Hades." Is this merely a poetic way of saying that at around forty you get terribly worried about dying?

Throughout this book, I have been working with several sets of materials and interweaving them around the theme of the midlife transition: the stories and images that cluster around the Greek god Hermes and around some other mythic figures, various anthropological studies on initiation and rites of passage, and the experience of midlife among individuals in contemporary Western society as studied and commented on by social scientists and as encountered in my own analytical practice. The phenomenon to keep an eye on is always psychological *transition*, a universally human experience found cross-culturally and in different age groups of both sexes. All of these materials are brought together, then, for the purpose of gaining insight into what is going on psychologically at midlife and particularly for exploring some of the less obvious features of the core of this experience, liminality.

But *how* are these materials related to each other? If the method of amplification were merely comparative and left off interpreting at the point of indicating a few commonalities among a group of essentially disparate materials, then indeed all it could produce would be a pretty thin sort of poetry. The product would be a simile, as in: "midlife death anxiety is like going to Hades." But amplification does not aim to create similes; it aims to expose unconscious meaning. And the methodology underlying it claims an altogether different kind of linkage among these materials than the sort of loosely horizontal type typical of the "comparison and contrast" method.

The argument is that a common archetype, located in the unconscious layers of the human psyche, underlies all of these materials: the mythic world of Hermes and Hades, the various cultural forms of initiatory rites of passage, and the contemporary experience among individuals of midlife transition and liminality. These are rooted vertically, not linked horizontally, in a common archetype. And this archetype governs the pattern, albeit somewhat flexibly and modified by individual and cultural influences, of this psychologically transitional period—its timing, its dynamic movement and its stages, and its contents of image, perception, feeling, ideation, somatic manifestation, and synchronistic event. A specific archetype, then, forms and informs this piece of a person's life experience and history.

The goal of the amplification method is to expose this archetype to view as much as possible. Through my gathering together the various phenomena produced by it, each piece of which is at least a partial or opaque reflection of it, evidence appears of its structure and dynamics and of its place in the overall life pattern. As science, this method results in a kind of ethological study of human behavior, describing general inherited patterns of human psychological functioning (cf. 1976, §1228). At a more practical existential level, it aims to elucidate the functioning of archetypes within the psychological life of individuals, to discover meaning, and to provide orientation and understanding that can be cashed out pragmatically. At both levels, however, the potential value of this method depends on getting through the surfaces of the related materials, in order at least to come close to what they are commonly rooted in, a factor that Jung called their "unconscious core of meaning" (1959a, §266).

The archetype we are dealing with in considering the experience of a deep-going psychological transformation at midlife is the same as operates in all other transitional periods of life. It is reflected in images of the edge, of boundary lines and borderlines, thresholds, in-between spaces and times. And persons whose consciousness is caught up in the force field of this archetype of transition, whenever it occurs, experience liminality with its characteristic and often predictable fantasies, feelings, visions, dreams, and even synchronistic events. Mythic imagination saw a master of this mode of existence, of liminality, in Hermes and called him guide of souls and god of thresholds and of passages between realms of existence. So when we say that Hermes is present in a situation what we are saying, to put it more pedantically, is that the archetype that was imaged in the mythic figure Hermes is active in this situation as well and is creating these effects.

But of the depths of liminality itself there are other images: of death, of Hades, of human suffering like Job's and Jonah's, of the night sea journey, of *nigredo* in alchemy. So when we say that in midlife liminality there is a steep descent to Hades, we mean that an archetypal power draws consciousness into the pit of radical liminality. Here the world and all of existence appear insubstantial and ghostlike, futile, essentially not material, and inverted in values and priorities; here we seem fated to exact tasks, limits, and repetitions. Little wonder we feel anxiety at the prospect.

The practical purpose of looking to mythic images—figures, themes, geographies—is to provide orientation for consciousness. The imagination that saw Hermes' actions and filled the world of liminality with detail and drama shows us ways for moving in and dealing with the experience of radical liminality and for understanding its function. For this reason, we look to the myths of Hermes for guidance and protection and for clues on how to understand these periods of life and to move forward and through them.

As a method of psychotherapy and analysis rather than of scientific research, amplification of course begins and ends with the individual, with a single patient's subjective experience. Starting with the 'stuff' of a person's immediate psychological matrix—patterns of feeling and thought, images, dreams—amplification moves toward seeing the configuration of these elements against more explicitly archetypal patterns. The therapeutic object of this is to make the archetypal depths palpable, to open the visible surface of consciousness to the invisible presence of the archetypal extensions beyond it. There live the primal powers in each of us, the animals and the gods, the instincts and the spirit. It is to see and feel through to these presences in and around oneself that amplification is undertaken in analysis.

The object of this study, which is to explore the "unconscious core of meaning" of the midlife transition and of the experience of liminality within it, is different, then, from what mythologists like Kerényi aim for when they study myth. Kerényi's works describe mythic patterns and contribute to the study of the history of religions, and they also make ancient modes of thought and imagination accessible to modern consciousness. My object is different, too, from what sociologists and cultural anthropologists do when they study myth. These researchers and thinkers tend to place myth in the context of social and cultural patterns of meaning and behavior, in order to understand those societies and perhaps to find new perspectives on our own society as well. The method of amplification, on the contrary, employs myth to reveal archetypal patterns of psychological functioning and to elucidate the meaning of psychological events in the lives of contemporary individuals, on the argument that individual persons today are psychologically rooted in the same collective and archetypal patterns of the psyche as were the ancients and primitive peoples who personified these patterns in the form of myth. These objectives make my work different from Kerényi's, on the one hand, and from Turner's on the other, while this argument is the justification for using their explorations of myth and cultural pattern to carry my work forward.

In returning from this methodological side street to the chapter's main theme, I turn to the image of Hades and the account of Odysseus's journey to this land of the dead as an amplification for elucidating the nadir of liminality at midlife, its deepest and most critical moment. What is this piece of the psychological pattern of midlife transition like descriptively? What is the archetype operative in this experience? And what is its psychological meaning and function within a person's life as a whole? These are the questions I will contend with in the remainder of this chapter.

Hades, the realm of dead souls, represents the experience of liminality *in extremis*. Here the soul exists as a shade, a pure form or image (*eidolon*) without material substance. This is a form of existence that is also a kind of non-existence. In the *Odyssey*, Hades is the furthest Odysseus wanders on his journey from Troy to his home in Ithaka; it is the far point of his Hermetic journeying. Similarly, in Christian symbolism Christ's descent to hell during his liminal existence between his crucifixion and resurrection marks the far point of his journey from the divine world into the realm of the human condition. If Hades is not necessarily the most dangerous place Odysseus visits during his wanderings, it is certainly the most depressing, and unlike Christ's journey to hell it has nothing of the heroic about it.

By linking this image, Hades, to our understanding of the liminal phase of the midlife transition, it may be possible to come closer to the "unconscious core of meaning" within this midlife experience. We know that liminality is a central feature of initiation rituals and rites of passage, the time during which the deepest transformations occur. Hades is closely associated with themes of transformation, because even though nothing happens in Hades itself, which is imagined as an absolute endpoint, this image touches on, and leads to the functioning of, the deeper archetypal pattern of death and rebirth. It is the specific function and meaning of *this* archetype at midlife, as distinguished from its action during other transformational phases of the life span, that concerns us here.

Whenever the image of Hades or its equivalent—the underworld, hell, Sheol, the far side of the moon, etc.—appears in dreams and fantasies or as the best imaginal representation of a current state of consciousness, the condition of liminality is indicated. This image, above all others, is a litmus test for the presence of liminality. What its appearance means in a particular instance, however, depends on a number of factors and on the relations among them: age, immediate social and family circumstance, recent events, various psychodynamically determinative structures and forces. This image of liminality may, for example, symbolize narcissistic or borderline fragmentation, or severe depressive reaction, or schizoid withdrawal, or other pathological states and conditions. In practice, therefore, the appearance of this image in an individual's psychological material must be placed within a personal context. Midlife, and the experience of midlife transition, is one of the times and places it can and does appear.

The account of Odysseus and his companions sailing to Hades offers a detailed image of the landscape of this experience of liminality:

> '... Circe
> of the lovely hair, the dread goddess, who talks with mortals,
> sent us an excellent companion, a following wind, filling
> the sails, to carry from astern the ship with the dark prow.
> We ourselves, over all the ship making fast the running gear,
> sat still, and let the wind and the steersman hold her steady.
> All day long her sails were filled as she went through the water,
> and the sun set, and all the journeying-ways were darkened.
> She made the limit, which is of the deep-running Ocean.
> There lie the community and city of Kimmerian people,
> hidden in fog and cloud, nor does Helios, the radiant
> sun, ever break through the dark, to illuminate them with his
>   shining,
> neither when he climbs up into the starry heaven,
> nor when he wheels to return again from heaven to earth,
> but always a glum night is spread over wretched mortals.'
>
> (11: 5–19)

It is not unimportant to notice the landscapes of liminality, for they represent essential aspects and qualities of the experience. Victor Turner, the contemporary anthropologist who has powerfully reintroduced the concept of liminality into the current intellectual discussion, points out that because

> neophytes are ... structurally "invisible" (though physically visible) and ritually polluting, they are very commonly secluded, partially or completely, from the realm of culturally defined and ordered states

and statuses. Often the indigenous term for the liminal period is, as among Ndembu, the locative form of a noun meaning "seclusion site" (*kunkunka, kung'ula*). The neophytes are sometimes said to "be in another place." They have physical but not social "reality," hence they have to be hidden, since it is a paradox, a scandal, to see what ought not to be there! Where they are not removed to a sacred place of concealment they are often disguised, in masks or grotesque costumes or striped with white, red, or black clay, and the like. (1967, p. 98)

The mythic realm of Hades is such "another place," a place of deep invisibility and isolation. It describes a region of psychological existence, removed from the domain of standard social and psychological structures, of darkness and insubstantiality, where all souls inevitably must go. It is a place made up purely of psyches, of pure psychic existence.

Turner carries out his fascinating and highly suggestive discussion of liminality largely by using the concepts of social classification and of interstructural phases between socially classificatory categories. Liminality occurs in the time between social classifications, as a person is passing from one social status to another. In his view, therefore, the experience of liminality is primarily a social experience. But these social concepts have psychological equivalents, and for my purposes a translation of them into psychological concepts is necessary. The classificatory social categories themselves correspond to the stable structures in an individual's psychological makeup and life history that are rooted in unconscious dominant patterns of self-organization (the archetypes), and, like social categories, these structure consciousness and a person's experience in ways that produce strong and certain feelings of identity. The interstructural phases correspond to periods of psychological flux and turmoil when the dominant patterns are undergoing deep change, when formerly repressed or unrealized aspects of the Self are gaining more prominence, and when social position and status are consequently often insufficient to maintain a sense of identity. During a period of psychological liminality, socially defined identity becomes a 'mere persona,' merely a superficial mask to hide behind or to use for enacting a hollow role in society.

From the viewpoint of this psychological perspective, collective rituals such as "rites of passage" have their source and *raison d'etre* in the psychological needs of individuals and are indeed developed in order to accommodate them. Psychological facts, therefore, such as an individual's identity and the dominants of an individual's consciousness, are not by-products of social structuring and categorizing, although they are not totally independent of social forces and categories either. The relation between the psychological needs and dynamics and structures of the individuals forming a culture and the shaping forces of the social forms and role expectations of their cultural milieux must be seen as reciprocal, but psyche is primary. Social customs, patterns, and rituals are expressions of, or containers for, the various aspects of the psyche's dynamics, archetypal patterns and forms, and purposes. I do not claim *immediate* psychological causation of social dynamics and structures, but I do put forward the claim that the psyche is their *first* cause and their *final* cause.

Anthropological studies such as those of Turner and van Gennep, which do not in any manner share this viewpoint, do nevertheless provide data for establishing the archetypal nature of an individual's psychological experience. Not only do these studies show and help to establish the cross-cultural aspects and general forms of specific human experiences, they also, like images of myth, provide material for amplifying them and therefore for exploring the "unconscious core of meaning" behind or within an individual's life experience.

So I turn to Turner's detailed anthropological studies of liminality to amplify the experience of midlife liminality among contemporary individuals. "The symbolism attached to and surrounding the liminal *persona* is complex and bizarre," Turner writes.

The structural "invisibility" of liminal *personae* has a twofold character. They are at once no longer classified and not yet classified. In so far as they are no longer classified, the symbols that represent them are, in many societies, drawn from the biology of death, decomposition, catabolism, and other physical processes that have a negative tinge, such as menstruation (frequently regarded as the absence or loss of a fetus). . . . In so far as a neophyte is structurally "dead," he or she may be treated, for a long or short period, as a corpse is customarily treated in his or her society. (See Stobaeus' quotation, probably from a lost work of Plutarch, "initiation and death correspond word for word and thing for thing." [James 1961, p. 132]) The neophyte may be buried, forced to lie motionless in the posture and direction of customary burial, may be stained black, or may be forced to live for a while in the company of masked and monstrous mummers representing, *inter alia*, the dead, or worse still, the un-dead. The metaphor of dissolution is often applied to neophytes; they are allowed to go filthy and identified with the earth, the generalized matter into which every specific individual is rendered down. Particular form here becomes general matter; often their very names are taken from them and each is called solely by the generic term for "neophyte" or "initiand." (1967, p. 96)

In this region of the "no longer classified and the not yet classified," we find loss of personal identity and the coalescence of images of tomb and womb: images of corpses and ghosts come together with images of embryos and neophytes. For now, however, the focus is on images of death and decomposition. In the passage quoted from Turner, there occurs the intriguing sentence from Stobaeus: "initiation and death correspond word for word and thing for thing." Imagery of death and decomposition seems to be uniquely suited to what happens during initiation and the experience of liminality. By looking to the Greek image of Hades, a radical image of death and the dead, we are looking at the core of this experience. For this, myth and religion may be more helpful than observations of ritual, because myth, like the dream, provides a self-portrait of a deeply invisible and perhaps ultimately unknowable process in the deepest unconscious regions of the psyche, and religious experience and thought are derived from this same region.

Turner alludes several times to the rites and initiations that were a part of the Greek Eleusinian and Orphic mysteries. Orphism, especially, both as a religious philosophy and practice, provides a doorway to the inner vision of liminality and to the perspective it offers. Orphism's teachings represent an attitude toward life and death that expresses the essence of liminality's vision, which is also imaged by the realm of Hades. The Orphic practitioner looked at life and at conscious experience from within the experience of liminality. Nilsson points out that Orphism inverted the categories of life and death as these had been understood by Homer and would even today be understood by 'normal' perception and conceptions of life and death and by common sense. He writes:

> ... Plato mentions the doctrine that the body is the tomb of the soul, in which it lies buried during life, and adds that the Orphics call it so because the soul is shut up in the body as in a prison. The Homeric conception of the living body as the man himself and the soul as a pale, lifeless shadow is completely inverted. How this total inversion was possible we can understand from a passage in Pindar. The body, he says, follows mighty death, but the soul abides, which alone comes from the gods. The soul, he continues, sleeps while the limbs are busy, but when men sleep it shows the future in dreams. The meaning is that, as dreams are sent by the gods and the soul is divine, the soul must be free from the confinement of the body to experience the divine, that is, dreams. A similar view is met with again in the stories of extraordinary men whose soul soared free while the body lay in a trance. . . . (P. 24)

The Orphic doctrine of the transmigration of souls represents a further expression of liminal experience and of its sense of psychic reality. When the soul leaves the body it inhabits during this life, it goes into an unembodied existence where it continues to live until, for further testing or punishment, it is sent back to this side again and into another body. The process of transmigration is a process of the soul's purification and testing, and it comes to an end when the soul is released from this cycle of birth and rebirth because it has refrained from unrighteousness for three consecutive migrations. The soul is fundamental, the body incidental. ''An inversion of this life and the other took place,'' Nilsson summarizes, ''and thus we can explain the paradox that the body is the grave of the soul. As the soul is freed when the body dies, and goes into the other world, so it is confined in the prison of the body when it is sent up into this world again.'' (p. 25).

Orphism, as a religion of liminality, shows how palpable the soul becomes during liminality, and as the sense of psychic reality increases, the sense of the material world's importance declines. The valence of the object world leaks away as the experience of *psychological* reality—the dream, the image from the unconscious, the sense of a ''subtle body'' that gives expression to the psyche somatically—waxes in strength and vividness. Consensual social reality, too, loses its power to convince, and the rigor of social role expectations to govern ideals and behavior goes flaccid. A person in liminality has 'dropped out,' 'gone away' to ''another place,'' 'disappeared' into social and psychological invisibility. Here a radical sort of introversion and immersion in the unconscious has taken place, and the inner world consequently becomes more real and charged with energy than the outer adaptive context. Experience of the world of inner objects becomes more important, and the relationship among these inner objects—the imagos, the figures of persons and the textures of places remembered and imagined, the faces and drama of the complexes and archetypes—assumes a degree of fascination and importance above the concern for interpersonal relationships or the demands from an external adaptive context.

Turner comments suggestively about a possible cultural function of liminality: ''We have no way of knowing whether primitive initiations merely conserved lore. Perhaps they also generated new thought and new custom'' (1967, p. 97). His suggestion that something new may be generated during liminality, that it is a period of profound, if often obscure, creativity, can be affirmed on an individual level by many psychotherapists who have worked with persons in midlife liminality. Liminality is a womb after it is a tomb.

The ''journey to Hades'' episode in the *Odyssey* clearly demonstrates this point and amplifies it further. Hades is a place of the dead, but Odysseus gains two pieces of information there that are to have very far-reaching effects on the remainder of his life: negatively, he acquires a precise knowledge of limits; positively, he receives a long-range life task. This combination, the knowledge of limits and the conviction of a future life task, constitutes the essence of a meaningful recovery from the experience of midlife liminality. It is a product of this initiation, and a person's future sense of identity and purpose is based on it.

At the end of the Circe episode, Odysseus and his companions face the awesome task of sailing to Hades, there to consult Teiresias about the remainder of their voyage home. The progression of figures from Circe to Teiresias I read psychologically as a movement from the anima (who, Jung says [1961, p. 191], ''establishes a relationship to the collectivity of the dead; for the unconscious corresponds to the mythic land of the dead, the land of the ancestors'') to the wise old man, a figure who embodies wisdom and ''superior insight'' (ibid., p. 183).

Teiresias symbolizes wisdom. Blinded by a Great Goddess, Hera, for taking the side of Zeus in an argument about sexual pleasure, Teiresias was given ''second sight,'' the ability to see beyond surfaces to what is invisible and unconscious for others. His knowledge is knowledge of the unconscious. (It was Teiresias who revealed the truth about Oedipus's pollution.) This figure, then, represents knowledge of unconscious patterns and facts; his vision is directed toward the invisible, toward psyche.

Teiresias is an equivalent figure to the one Jung describes in his autobiography as Philemon:

> It was he who taught me psychic objectivity, the reality of the psyche. Through him the distinction was clarified between myself and the object of my thought. He confronted me in an objective manner, and I understood that there is something in me which can say things that I do not know and do not intend, things which may even be directed against me. (1961, p. 183)

Through the image (*eidolon*) of a Teiresias, or a Philemon, the Self speaks to persons who have ventured to the heart of liminality.

In the meeting between Odysseus and Teiresias, we have a parallel to Jung's confrontation with Philemon, a figure of the unconscious who represents wisdom, objectivity, and contact with the source of psychological truth and knowledge. It is his role to initiate the neophyte into the next stage of life and the next level of consciousness. The scene of this meeting from the Eleventh Book of the *Odyssey* is one of the most impressive moments in all of Western literature:

> 'Now came the soul of Teiresias the Theban, holding
> a staff of gold, and he knew who I was, and spoke to me:
> "Son of Laertes and seed of Zeus, resourceful Odysseus,
> how is it then, unhappy man, you have left the sunlight
> and come here, to look on dead men, and this place without pleasure?
> Now draw back from the pit, and hold your sharp sword away from
>   me,
> so that I can drink of the blood and speak the truth to you."
> 'So he spoke, and I, holding away the sword with the silver
> nails, pushed it back in the sheath, and the flawless prophet,
> after he had drunk the blood, began speaking to me.
> "Glorious Odysseus, what you are after is sweet homecoming,
> but the god will make it hard for you. I think you will not
> escape the Shaker of the Earth, who holds a grudge against you

in his heart, and because you blinded his dear son, hates you.
But even so and still you might come back, after much suffering,
if you can contain your own desire, and contain your companions',
at that time when you first put in your well-made vessel
at the island Thrinakia, escaping the sea's blue water,
and there discover pasturing the cattle and fat sheep
of Helios, who sees all things, and listens to all things.
Then, if you keep your mind on homecoming, and leave these
        unharmed,
you might all make your way to Ithaka, after much suffering;
but if you do harm them, then I testify to the destruction
of your ship and your companions, but if you yourself get clear,
you will come home in bad case, with the loss of all your companions,
in someone else's ship, and find troubles in your household,
insolent men, who are eating away your livelihood
and courting your godlike wife and offering gifts to win her.
You may punish the violences of these men, when you come home.
But after you have killed these suitors in your own palace,
either by treachery, or openly with the sharp bronze,
then you must take up your well-shaped oar and go on a journey
until you come where there are men living who know nothing
of the sea, and who eat food that is not mixed with salt, who never
have known ships whose cheeks are painted purple, who never
have known well-shaped oars, which act for ships as wings do.
And I will tell you a very clear proof, and you cannot miss it.
When, as you walk, some other wayfarer happens to meet you,
and says you carry a winnow-fan on your bright shoulder,
then you must plant your well-shaped oar in the ground, and render
ceremonious sacrifice to the lord Poseidon,
one ram and one bull, and a mounter of sows, a boar pig,
and make your way home again and render holy hecatombs
to the immortal gods who hold the wide heaven, all
of them in order. Death will come to you from the sea, in
some altogether unwarlike way, and it will end you

in the ebbing time of a sleek old age. Your people
about you will be prosperous. All this is true as I tell you.''

(11: 90–137)

Odysseus receives from Teiresias both a prohibition and a mission: on the one hand, he must withstand the temptation to satisfy his hunger by thieving and slaughtering the cattle and sheep of Helios; on the other hand, he must carry a ship's oar so far inland that people do not recognize it and there plant it in honor of Poseidon. Thus he is instructed to honor the claims of the dominant of collective consciousness (the sun god, Helios) and also to serve the formerly neglected dominant of the collective unconscious (the sea god, Poseidon).

(Parenthetically, the prohibition placed on Helios's cattle proves too much for Odysseus's starving companions. In their extreme hunger, they slaughter the animals while Odysseus is asleep, and for this they are struck by lightning in their ships and drowned. Odysseus narrowly escapes on a raft of splinters from the fragmented ship.)

The new state of consciousness that emerges from a prolonged experience of midlife liminality contains a dual sense of key limits and larger purposes and tasks. Both aspects of this attitude are backed by a religious sensibility that bears their import and meaning: the prerogatives of collective consciousness and the demands of the collective unconscious are recognized and honored as derived from 'the gods.' There is a sense that both are backed by archetypal powers.

In his autobiography, Jung describes this complex combination of attitudes in more personal psychological language. When he had completed his period of confrontation with the unconscious, at the age of forty-three, he emerged with a strong conviction that what he had learned from this experience carried an ethical imperative both to serve the needs of collective consciousness (culture) in his time and also to honor the unconscious daimon that had plagued and haunted him since his early childhood. "It is . . . a grave mistake," he writes, "to think that it is enough to gain some understanding of the images and that knowledge can here make a halt. Insight into them must be converted into an ethical obligation" (1961, pp. 192–93). This represents an ethical commitment to shape life according to the limitations and challenges that are imposed by the insights won during the initiatory descent. These work together to produce an inner sense of direction and meaning. Jung's retrospective reflection on the meaning of his midlife experience of liminality, given some forty-five years after the event, summarizes this point:

> When I look back upon it all today and consider what happened to me during the period of my work on the fantasies, it seems as though a message had come to me with overwhelming force. There were things in the images which concerned not only myself but many others also. It was then that I ceased to belong to myself alone, ceased to have the right to do so. From then on, my life belonged to the generality. The knowledge I was concerned with, or was seeking, still could not be found in the science of those days. I myself had to undergo the original experience, and, moreover, try to plant the results of my experience in the soil of reality; otherwise they would have remained subjective assumptions without validity. It was then that I dedicated myself to service of the psyche. I loved it and hated it, but it was my greatest wealth. My delivering myself over to it, as it were, was the only way by which I could endure my existence and live it as fully as possible. (1961, p. 192)

Jung describes his sense of mission—"to plant the results of my experience in the soil of reality"—with an agricultural metaphor that is not far removed from the task given to Odysseus, to plant an oar, the emblem of his experience on the waters of the unconscious, in a land where others had never heard of the sea (in Jung's time, the scientific community). This mission obliges Odysseus to honor his experience on the sea, to give it expression, and to symbolize it for others. This is not necessarily a missionary impulse, although that impulse may also be rooted in the imperative to bear visible testimony to inner experience. Odysseus's mission was to show forth the emblem of the god who had plagued his existence the most: Poseidon Earthshaker, Lord of the Deeps. For Jung, this god was the psyche itself, which was for him a numinous daimon of creativity (cf. Jaffé). Jung emerged from his midlife transition with a singular commitment to psyche.

In an earlier chapter, I quoted the classical scholar Onians as saying that for the ancient Greeks the ''soul'' (*psyché*) lay dormant while a person was awake and busy dealing with the world, coping, adapting, etc. The soul came awake only during sleep and at death. This view is much like the inversion of attitude and perspective on life that Orphism exemplified, with its reversal of values and of the 'normal' sense of reality, the dream and the 'other world' gaining in reality at the expense of the material, everyday, bodily world. What seems to come to fuller consciousness during midlife liminality is similarly an awareness of *psyché*, of the subjective factor in the background of our experience, the soul that is otherwise dormant and invisible in the bright light of waking consciousness. Consciousness of soul, or soul-consciousness, seems to be the chief product of midlife liminality.

With this in mind, and recalling, too, that the Greek words for soul and for butterfly are identical (both are expressed by the word *psyché*), I present the dream of a woman who found herself in the depths of midlife liminality. She knew nothing consciously about the psychological meaning of the symbolism in her dream. I regard this dream as paradigmatic of the experience of midlife liminality and of its distant outcome.

> I am walking along a road, feeling depressed. Suddenly I stumble on a gravestone and look down to see my own name on it. At first I am

shocked, but then strangely relieved. I find myself trying to get the corpse out of the coffin but realize that I am the corpse. It is becoming more and more difficult to hold myself together because there is nothing much left to keep the body together anymore.

I go through the bottom of the coffin and enter a long dark tunnel. I continue until I come to a small, very low door. I knock. An extremely old man appears and says: "So you have finally come." (I notice he is carrying a staff with two snakes entwined around it, facing one another.) Quietly but purposefully he brings out yards and yards of Egyptian linen and wraps me from head to foot in it, so I look like a mummy. Then he hangs me upside down from one of many hooks on the low ceiling and says: "You must be patient, it's going to take a long time."

Inside the cocoon it's dark and I can't see anything that is happening. At first, my bones hold together, but later I feel them coming apart. Then everything becomes liquid. I know that the old man has put one snake in at the top and one at the bottom, and they are moving from top to bottom, and back and forth from side to side, making figure eights.

Meanwhile I can see the old man sitting at a window, looking out on the seasons as they pass. I see winter come and go; then spring, summer, fall, and winter again. Many seasons go by. In the room there is nothing but me in this cocoon with the snakes, the old man, and the window open to the seasons.

Finally the old man unwraps the cocoon. There is a wet butterfly. I ask: "Is it very big or is it small?"

"Both," he answers. "Now we must go to the sunroom to dry you out."

We go to a large room with a big circle cut out of the top. I lie on the circle under this to dry out, while the old man watches over the process. He tells me that I am not to think of the past or the future, but to "just be here and be still."

Finally he leads me to the door and says: "When you leave you can go in all four directions, but you are to live in the middle."

Now the butterfly flies up into the air. Then it descends to the earth and comes down on a dirt road. Gradually it takes on the head and body of a woman, and the butterfly is absorbed, and I can feel it and see it inside my chest.

Chapter Seven

On the Road of Life After Midlife

> Hermes, for to you beyond all other gods it is
> dearest
> to be man's companion . . .
>
> *Iliad*

Throughout these reflections on Hermes and the soul at midlife, I have touched only lightly on the role of Hermes as companion. While giving considerable detail to several of his functions—as *guide* (through the defenses to the corpse that needs to be retrieved and buried), as *thief* (of a 'brother's' property), as *protector* (against possession by the power of a goddess)—I have not focused on this other classic aspect of Hermes as friend and companion to humankind. In this final chapter, I shall give specific attention to this side of Hermes, for the key value that can be derived from this period of crisis and turmoil is a religious attitude: the continuing consciousness—once the midlife transition has been completed—of Hermes' presence in a person's life.

Kerényi concludes his inspired study of Hermes with the sentence: "For all to whom life is an adventure—whether an adventure of love or of spirit—he is the common guide. *Koinos Hermes!*" (1976, p. 91). These final words are intended to distill an essential feature of Hermes, and they indicate the mythic core around which this chapter's reflections will revolve.

What does Kerényi mean by *koinos* Hermes? The Greek adjective *koinos* means 'common, shared in common . . . common to all the people, public' (Common Hermes). It can also indicate 'commonness,' in the sense of something mean or profane or even vulgar (Vulgar Hermes). The Greek in which the New Testament was written, for example, is called *koine* Greek, a somewhat vulgar dialect of the common people. In relation to the state and the *polis*, *koinos* is a noun meaning 'commonwealth,' that which is held in common by everyone in the community and belongs to all persons in it equally (Common Property Hermes). So what Kerényi must intend with this final salute to Hermes is to indicate Hermes' general availability to everyone: "For *all* to whom life is an adventure . . . he is the *common* guide." Hermes is not of the elite, whether social or cultural, intellectual or religious, any more than we would think today of the guiding, thieving, soul-tending, and protecting unconscious as inaccessible to *anyone* for whom life is an adventure. . . .

Koinos has another meaning, and this one may be the most pertinent to our consideration of Hermes as companion on the road into, through, and beyond midlife liminality. When this adjective is used in relation to persons, it indicates someone who is 'impartial, affable, accessible.' And when the Greeks attached the suffix *tays* to it, they created a noun, *koinotays*, meaning both 'affability' and 'sharing in common, fellowship.' So as applied to Hermes ("*Koinos* Hermes!"), this epithet indicates a Hermes who is accessible and companionable, a god who brings fellowship into a human encounter and the quality of community into a group.

It happens often that two people who are on the road either literally or metaphorically will meet in this liminal space and experience Hermes' presence: an unusually intense atmosphere of intimacy is suddenly created between them. First one will lead, then the other, as the thread of conversation rushes by in a flurry of suggestive but unfinished thoughts and subtle gestures, which take them all the while deeper and pull them closer. Feelings of immediacy, of connecting, of being joined by common bonds and ties of spiritual kinship spring up, and there appears a surprisingly vital potential for sharing deeply this piece of life's journey. Psyche pours out in the form of stories, secrets, wishes, fantasies, dreams, memories, and the flow of it passes along unhindered by what would otherwise be unbridgeable distances in social class, geographical place or origin, age, educational level, and psychological typology. This communicating can flow through many channels—by way of mouth, hand, eye. And is it not one of our most persistent hopes and fantasies to find, somewhere out there on the road, a fellow journeyer and soul companion? It must be that we are unconsciously looking for Hermes, for the communion this archetype brings us when we are together in the liminality of the road. The resemblance of what transpires psychologically in this space to what is called transference in psychotherapy is not accidental: Hermes is the god of transference.

The wish for Hermes' companionship has two strands: one is the wish for journeying itself, for being on a journey, and the other is a wish for intense intimacy and communion. "His companions are the companions of the journey," Kerényi writes; "not those he wants to lead home, as Odysseus his comrades, but those he joins. . . .With companions of the journey, one experiences openness to the extent of purest nakedness, as though he who is on the journey had left behind every stitch of clothing or covering" (p. 14). Journeying Hermetically implies this deep form of communion, of the "purest nakedness." This type of radical and unabashed intimacy is one of the hallmarks of the realm of Hermes. To experience life and the world within the boundaries of this archetype is to experience existence "on the road" and to discover there the primacy of human companionship and the mutuality that exists between naked souls.

"For communitas," Victor Turner writes, "has an existential quality; it involves the whole man in his relation to other whole men.'' Turner places great weight on the point that liminality invariably includes the experience of *communitas* among the persons who are together in it, in contrast to the hierarchically structured social relationships that pertain under other conditions. ''Structure . . . has cognitive quality,'' he continues; ''as Lévi-Strauss has perceived, it is essentially a set of classifications, a model for thinking about culture and nature and ordering one's public life. Communitas has also an aspect of potentiality; it is often in the subjunctive mood. Relations between total beings are generative of symbols and metaphors and comparisons; art and religion are their products rather than legal and political structures'' (1969, pp. 127–28).

Turner quotes Martin Buber, the great modern-day Hebrew poet-prophet, on community: '''Community is the being no longer side by side (and, one might add, above and below) but *with* one another of a multitude of persons. And this multitude, though it moves towards one goal, yet experiences everywhere a turning to, a dynamic facing of, the others, a flowing from *I* to *Thou*''' (p. 127). In the communities created by persons coming together in and through the experience of liminality, side-by-side and one-up one-down positions are absent, then, and instead we find a ''flowing from I to Thou,'' companionability, and the generation of symbol and metaphor: a collective epiphany of Hermes.

While Turner emphasizes the element of communitas within groups of liminal personae, Kerényi adduces the mating journey of two lovers as the core experience of Hermes' companionship. The honeymoon trip, in his view, amplifies the central features of the Hermetic journey and the kind of intimate companionship that occurs in liminal time and space.

Buber must have had a similar model in mind, however, for defining and describing the I-Thou relationship: his conception can be accurately pictured as two journeying soul-lovers intimately imagining, and helping the other to imagine, the reality of the whole psychological person. The I-Thou relation mingles subjects, subject-to-subject in a field of total subjectivity, where all important objects in the world have subjective value and significance and continue existing in this field only for that reason.

This, too, is what Kerényi implies with his reference to the honeymoon trip. But, like Turner, he places the experience essentially outside the structures of normal social life, an accent that is not quite so strong in Buber. "Do not today those who wish to be free of the bonds to the community in which they grew up and to which they were intimately bound," Kerényi writes, "and who want to be open to each other without reservation or boundary, as two naked souls —do they not go on a wedding journey (*Hochzeitsreise*)?" (1976, p. 14). Here the wish for freedom from social constraints, the experience of liminality, and radical intimacy converge in what we would call the honeymoon trip.

The honeymoon trip is of course a venture into liminality, falling betwixt-and-between statuses and identities, and so it takes place in the psychological domain where the whole range of liminal experience is available. The emotional valency of a honeymoon trip can as easily swing toward images of a descent to the underworld, as in the mythic seizure of Persephone by Hades and their ensuing wedding journey to the land of the dead, as toward an I-Thou passage through strange lands and pleasing consciousness-altering times. It may be, or suddenly turn into, an uncanny period of emotional upheaval and intense turmoil or a time of tender companionship and naked intimacy. Hermes is implicated in both ends of this spectrum, in the one as thief and trickster, in the other as bringer of transference and of soul-to-soul communion. Kerényi fuses these two aspects of Hermes' presence in the sentence that follows the passage just cited: "Is this journey not a '*Heimführung*' ('taking home' the bride) as well as an '*Entführung*' ('elopement'), and therefore also 'hermetic'?'' (ibid.).

Heimführung, or taking home a bride, refers to an ancient Greek practice, also displayed by other peoples, of bride-thieving, where the men of one tribe would stage raids on other tribes, usually at night, for the purpose of stealing women and making them their brides. Norman O. Brown comments on this type of thieving in connection with his study of Hermes, and writes as follows:

> Primitive communities go beyond their own boundaries to seek not only material goods but also wives. And since the transference of women from one family group to another is beset with the same dangers and difficulties as the transference of property, the conventions surrounding marriage are similar to those governing trade. Bride-seizure, of which there are vestiges in Greek marriage customs, follows the same pattern as exchange by mutual permission to steal; it is a formality observed even when the marriage has the consent of the bride's family. In the age of village communities the festivals on the boundary were the great occasion for mating as well as for trade: hence the tradition of sexual license at these festivals even in classical times. "Stealing" a strange woman was a magical act consummated in the rituals on the boundary. Thus Hermes came to be the master of the magic art of seduction and a patron god of marriage. (Pp. 43–44)

Kerényi's word *Heimführung* alludes to this scene of the captured bride being led home, and this trip is a Hermetic event, especially if the bride has been rendered cooperative and comes willingly. For then Hermetic magic has taken effect, because the bride has been seduced. This is a second meaning of Kerényi's other word, *Entführung*. On the one hand, it means 'elopement,' two lovers stealing away together in the night and going on a honeymoon trip without the blessing of family or community. But it can have nothing to do with marriage and mean simply 'seduction,' being the magical action by which one lover charms away the resistance of the other and gently persuades him or her to succumb to an unconscious desire, without implying a dependable future by hearth and home. *Entführung* can therefore also mean 'to be led astray,' and here Hermes plays the trickster. The winding path of the Hermetic journey can suddenly vanish or become a dead end ("Little is the profit he brings, and he beguiles endlessly / the tribes of mortal men throughout the night" [*Hymn*, 577-78]). Ambiguity and complexity define the Hermetic journey, and the qualities of it and its outcome are largely unpredictable. We may think we are being led home when we are actually only being taken for a ride.

The ambiguities that are a part of liminality and of the honeymoon trip add texture, if not seemingly outright contradiction, to Kerényi's observation that "Journeying is the best condition for loving" (ibid.). "Journeying," in Kerényi's sense of the honeymoon trip, is a passage in and through liminality and is different from "travelling." Merchants, statesmen, tourists "travel"; liminal personae "journey." Kerényi writes:

> ... we must ... imagine the often experienced reality of "journeying" as something very special. ... Odysseus is not a "traveller." He is a "journeyer". ... not simply because of his moving from place to place, but because of his existential situation. The traveller, despite his motion, adheres to a solid base, albeit one that is not narrowly circumscribed. With each step, he takes possession of another piece of the earth. ... he remains always bound to a solid earth beneath his feet. ... At every hearth that he encounters he lays claim to a kind of native citizenship for himself. ... His guardian is not Hermes, but Zeus, the God of the widest horizon and the firmest ground. In contrast, the situation of the journeyer is defined by movement, fluctuation. To someone more deeply rooted, even to the traveler [*sic*], he appears to be always in flight. In reality, he makes himself vanish

("volatizes himself") to everyone, also to himself. Everything around him becomes to him ghostlike and improbable, and even his own reality appears to him as ghostlike. He is completely absorbed by movement, but never by a human community that would tie him down. (1976, pp. 13–14)

So it is not simply the act of traveling that defines the Hermetic journey and constitutes "the best condition for loving"; it is rather the state of liminality, for which "being on the road" is an exact image.

Kerényi's conception of "journeying," which is essentially the same as my idea of 'floating,' includes a sense of unreality and improbability. The journeyers, or floaters, feel ghostlike, even to themselves ("Am *I* doing this?"); they vanish from their stable friends and surroundings, go up into thin air ("volatize" themselves), and disappear emotionally; they avoid social commitments and obligations, evade responsibility, duck out, drift off, hide, vanish. These verbs characterize the moves of Hermes, and this is his world. But within this world, there occurs paradoxically a special occasion for loving and companionship, but for a kind of living that is itself unique and a kind of companionship that both reaches beyond collegiality in intensity and falls short of it in dependability.

What is the sense, then, of the statement that "journeying" is the "best condition for loving"? "The gorges over which the 'volatized one' passes like a ghost," Kerényi writes, "can be the abysses of unbelievable love affairs—Circe and Calypso islands and holes; they can be abysses also in the sense that there no chance exists for standing on firm ground, but only for further floating between life and death" (1976, p. 14). "Ghost" is equivalent to "soul," and in liminality the soul is awakened and released, so it happens that during this transitional period a person is led by Hermes and ventures into psychological regions that are otherwise unknown, inaccessible, or forbidden—"Circe and Calypso islands and holes." When the soul wakes up during liminality and comes loose from the bonds of attachment and loyalty to a traditional community, it shakes free as well from the somnolent effects of psychological habits, patterns, and identifications. A person is now able to experience the ''gorges'' and ''abysses'' of existence and to enter into ''unbelievable love affairs'' with other soul figures: persons who signify vast subjective meanings and carry projections of the archetypal unconscious, who often shine with numinosity, who portend healing and salvation. In this condition, transference is archetypal, and this lends loving its special gleaming intensity.

Archetypal transference extends also to the world at large. The world appears as one vast soul-field infiltrated from top to bottom with *anima*, an *anima mundi*. Every object and person in it is a soul figure and calls forth careful psychological scrutiny; each item evokes a sense of importance and symbolic significance far beyond what is calculated by persons who live only in the faded (persona) world of road signs, taxes, and pragmatic coping strategies. And while ''no chance exists for standing on firm ground'' in this Hermetic space, since ''firm ground'' is made out of identifications and commitments and attachments, the anxiety and insecurity inevitably generated by this condition are often counted as little against its positive religious value.

But when we go into liminality and into the world of Hermes, and stay there long enough for deep-going psychological transformation to take place, the psyche begins to compensate this state of consciousness with realizations of *its* one-sidedness and with a dawning awareness of the positive values of what has been left out and excluded from this world. Gradually, a balanced sense of the opposites comes to the surface, which is quite different from the black/white splitting that may have been necessary earlier to impel a person to enter the transition period fully. Such oppositions as journeying and the road vs. householding and the hearth; fluctuation, change,

novelty, volatility vs. steadiness, continuity, reliability, solidity; unbelievable love affairs and intense soulful mingling of subjectivities
vs. 'good enough' relationships and dependable commitments; personality vs. character show an increasingly balanced valence. There
is a demand now to release the tension of these oppositions not
through repressing one side of them but through integrating them.

Surely most of us feel drawn by the intensity of experience
available in the world of Hermes, even while we fear its side-effects
of insecurity, insubstantiality, and vulnerability. On the other hand,
we also feel drawn by the promise of security in being rooted in
household and hearth, even while we fear its imprisoning side-effects
of routine, boredom, and predictability. Is there any way to avoid
the seeming inevitability of having to settle down to a boring marriage after the adventure of courtship and of a Hermetic honeymoon
trip? Is midlife liminality only an evanescent experience without en-
during psychological value or transformative power on consciousness? Does Hermes get to stay?

Fortunately for a person's individuation, a prolonged experience
of liminality during the midlife transition prevents a full reversion to
the *status ante quo*. Some of the awareness gained during liminality
must come along as a person enters a new period of stability and
consolidation.

But how much? Here we come upon the key psychological problem and task of ''reintegration,'' the third phase of the midlife transition. When opposites such as those just cited are constellated, the
psyche is demanding wholeness. The ego's tendency, however, is to
solve the problem of the opposites and of the psychic tension they
create by accepting one side (and identifying with it) and rejecting
the other (and repressing it). This produces a conflict between the
Self, which is made up of opposites and desires their 'marriage,' and
the ego, which hates tension and seeks security and comfort through
defense, one-sidedness, and identification. So the key task in this

phase, when the opposites are pulling for the ego's allegiance with equal urgency and conviction, is to place the ego in the service of the Self, to ask it to endure the stress of a psychological alchemy that is trying to unite the opposites in an amalgam that will also be a totally new element—psychological 'gold'! This 'gold,' "our gold" as the alchemists named it, is the conscious presence of the Self within the everyday world of egoic existence.

Hermes stays, not as the dominant archetype of consciousness that he was in the period of liminality, but as a continually possible agent of psychological movement and change. The optimal outcome of the midlife transition, it seems to me, is the creation of a reworked, more psychologically inclusive, and consequently more complex conscious sense of identity: one that does not take the form of a lithic personality monument, however, but of a uniquely and firmly channeled flow of libido, that still allows room for the play of floating in liminality. The Greek practice of keeping an image of Hermes at the gate or in the doorway of a home suggests this attitude. The statue of Hermes in this place is an affirmation that the road is nearby even when you are at home and secured at the hearth, that journeying is *always* a possibility. So receptiveness to the psyche's permanently liminal condition and to the continual presence of Hermes is retained within this newly integrated attitude of consciousness.

But this is an ideal. The psychological danger in this third phase of the midlife transition is that liminality will be excluded too much in the architecture of identity and consciousness that is being built up during this period. These structures, which were minimal during the phase of liminality, are arising rapidly now, and they can seal off the unconscious to the extent that liminality is barely registered any longer. Certainties of attitude and opinion can harden to rigidity as a person leaves midlife and enters the years of mature adulthood. So one of the major psychological tasks of persons in the post-midlife era is to identify ways of staying effectively in touch with liminality, as much as this may go against the grain of their newly won structures. In the remainder of this chapter, I shall try to suggest some practical ways for doing this.

I worked earlier with the idea that whenever we experience liminality and are thrown into its turmoil and confusion, Hermes is near—as guide, as guardian, as the presence of the unconscious. Here I would like to expand this idea and suggest that whenever Hermes is present we are also in, or close to, liminality. So if we can identify the fleeting presence of Hermes during the periods of stability and structure in our lives, we can perhaps also more easily stay in touch with liminality and maintain an active dialectic between structure and liminality.

Where do we sense the presence of Hermes in everyday life? Dreams are, of course, the *locus classicus* of the activity of Hermes and of the appearance of liminality within all periods and phases of life. But there are many other events as well in which we can find the hand of Hermes at work. The ancient Greeks saw Hermes, for instance, in the lull of a conversation: when everybody stops talking, Hermes is passing through the room. So in the midst of the persona ploys and the status rankings of a social gathering, the liminal world of Hermes suddenly opens up, and the anxiety you feel is anxiety before the uncanny and the unexpected, before liminality. This type of sudden and passing darkness at noon is an epiphany of Hermes.

Imagine another scenario. You plan a trip. In advance you secure your passage, you purchase traveler's checks, you load yourself up with expensive luggage, you cover yourself with insurance policies, and you reserve hotel space three months in advance. Finally you set out, a traveler and a tourist, conspicuously not a journeyer. But the plane returns for repairs and runs hours late; the baggage gets misticketed to the other side of the world; you lose your traveler's check and they are *not* American Express, and the food makes you ill. The trickster Hermes is in charge, and you are journeying suddenly in liminality, not traveling comfortably over a solid surface to a certain goal. When the world defeats the ego, the soul can float; then fantasy and imagination, the unconscious, have a chance to enter the scene and be noticed.

In the Preface to her husband's study of Hermes, Magda Kerényi tells a story that illustrates the author's ability to spot Hermes in a situation of sudden change. "... Hermes could ... reveal his presence through contrariness," she writes and quotes an incident that Kerényi recorded in his diary:

> ... in the Isthmus Canal. The first time it was with Anatole France's *Révolte des Anges* in a Greek translation. . . . And now it is precisely Anatole France—in a not-as-good translation of *Thais*—that was again stolen from me, disappeared together with the chair I had reserved. . . . Does Hermes wish to play the same game with me again? In any event I am left with the feeling of being stolen from, something uncanny, a vague sense of change in circumstances—truly something hermetic. (1976, p. v)

Kerényi knew liminality and itinerancy well. A refugee from Hungary, he lived the life of a freelance scholar in Ascona, Switzerland, where he must often have felt both at home and abroad at the same time. So the "vague sense of change in circumstances," noted in his diary in 1952, ten years after he was allowed to leave his homeland and begin life in Switzerland, was probably a familiar feeling. It is a sense of Hermes' subtle presence in events and of nearby liminality.

What about married life as a possible locus for Hermes' epiphanies? Marriage is often counted as one of those stable institutions of traditional life that definitively exclude liminality from their jurisdictions. When two people get married, out the window goes the adventure of honeymoon journeying together through liminality, as the risks of intense intimacy are traded for the securities found in repeating family patterns. Archetypal transference is replaced by personal transference as the glue of the relationship. Unfortunately, this deadens marriage and creates the need to experience liminality and the world of Hermes (in some version of those "unbelievable love affairs") outside marital boundaries. Is it possible to be married differently after the midlife transition, in a way that retains an awareness of Hermes within the limits of a permanent monogamous relationship? Can marriage be the place where the structure/liminality dialectic is a centerpiece?

If the answer is "yes," then how to do it? The key lies in attending to the presence of Hermes within married life, and the responsibility for this rests squarely on the psychological attitude of the married individual, not on the system or on some assumed inherent 'nature' of the marriage relationship. Strategies for changing the marriage system by tinkering with the rules of the game, to make it more 'open,' may indeed introduce liminality but may as well have the effect of seriously undermining structure. You get liminality all right, but you lose marriage. Since the ego tends to resolve the tension of the opposites by identifying with one side or the other of a perceived polarity, one suspects that this choice of liminality over structure is mainly an ego ploy. This has obvious drawbacks as a technique for maintaining the structure/liminality dialectic in marriage.

More commonly, however, marriage induces a person to identify with the side of structure, and so a more frequently chosen option than the sacrifice of structure in marriage is the sacrifice of liminality. The assumption is that marriage, like the original family system, is supposed to exclude the chaos of life and therefore also exclude Hermes and the world of liminality. This assumption, which is a throwback to a child's naive view of the security afforded by marriage and family life, reflects the personal transference at work in marriage. When this is the case and the opportunity for sustaining the dialectic between structure and liminality comes up in marriage, it appears as an ego defeat: the ego's assumptions about protection and the power of structure over liminality are overthrown by events.

"What have you done with my keys?!" Let this stand for the typical reaction that occurs in married life when the ego of one partner is defeated by Hermes and is threatened with liminality. The irritation in this reaction stems from an ego defeat (I need my keys *now*! I want to go somewhere!), and the blaming reaction implies the assumption that the structures of marriage are supposed to insure a person against the accidents and confusion and troubles of life, against liminality. This transference-based reaction is also resistance to the presence of Hermes and to liminality. Hermes has entered the house like a thief and stolen your keys. You are tricked. You have unconsciously misplaced your keys, and by blaming your mate, you are condemning your own disorderliness. This is not only mistreatment of your mate but an attack on Hermes as well, and so you miss the chance of attending to the unconscious at work behind the scenes. Here the opportunity for including liminality within the structured existence of marriage has been missed.

When accidents and unconsciously determined events defeat the intentions of the ego, in whatever context of life this occurs, including marriage, Hermes is on the move and liminality is an immediate possibility that must be seized if this dialectic is to be sustained.

Aniela Jaffé describes the kind of attitude I am struggling to recommend. "Jung reacted in a manner I was to find typical of him," she writes in her book, *From the Life and Work of C. G. Jung* (p. 102).

We had set up a UFO Archive . . . consisting of numerous books and technical writings about UFO's, as well as photographs, newspaper clippings from all over the world, letters, reports of dreams, and Jung's own notes. They rapidly filled several bookshelves and five or six large files, which, for lack of space, I had to accommodate in two different drawers. One afternoon Jung could not find the picture of a UFO he wanted to show a visitor—an annoying but not particularly important incident. Since I was working that afternoon in my flat, it would have been quite easy for one of the house servants to telephone me, and in two sentences I would have put the matter right. But that way out would never have entered his head. Whenever in a similar impasse this convenient solution was suggested, he rejected it. This was not due to his dislike of the telephone and other modern gadgets, but to his basic attitude to everything that happened: he preferred to let things develop in their own way. "Don't interfere!" was one of his guiding axioms, which he observed so long as a waiting-and-watching attitude could be adopted without danger. . . . This attitude of Jung's was the very reverse of indolence; it sprang from a curiosity about life and events that is characteristic of the researcher. They happened and he let them happen, not turning his back on them but following their development with keen attention, waiting expectantly to see what would result. Jung never ruled out the possibility that life knew better than the correcting mind, and his attention was directed not so much to the things themselves as to that unknowable agent which organizes the event beyond the will and knowledge of man. His aim was to understand *the hidden intentions of the organizer*, and, to penetrate its secrets, no happening was too trivial and no moment too short-lived. (Italics added.)

This is how to honor Hermes and to retain his companionship within the structured realms of life. Hermes and liminality are near even when we are sitting behind desks, or at the hearth with a mate, or working in our own gardens.

It has been suggested that Jung (and Jungian analysts after him) promote permanent liminality as a psychological ideal (Homans, p. 208), which for this discussion would imply that there should be no renewal of psychological structure and no stable sense of identity after the midlife transition is completed. (Jung's view, they say, is that Odysseus should keep wandering the face of the earth forever.) Criticism based on this perception of the Jungian position would arise from students of his work who themselves favor a major commitment to collective institutions and ego adaptation to existing social forms. On the other side of the fence, Jungians have been accused of selling out to structure, of becoming overly committed to the development of consciousness and to ego adaptation to society and culture, of excluding liminality and Hermes too much. (Jung lets Odysseus develop a middle-age paunch, they assert.) This criticism comes from therapists and students who tend to the romantic and who possibly would present permanent liminality as an ideal.

It seems to me that if there have been Jungians who have gone toward one extreme of the polarity or the other, or if Jung himself, in his writings and personal life history, at times reflects more the one side than the other, it is because of the complexity of the Jungian position, which favors maintaining a vigorous dialectic between structure and liminality. When Jung advocates developing the "transcendent function," which is a psychological bridge of traffic between consciousness and the unconscious, or living the "symbolic life," which means sensing the archetypal dimensions within the patterns, actions, and choices of everyday life, he is speaking for this dialectical relationship between structure and liminality. And this is what I propose as the ideal outcome of the midlife transition.

As the midlife transition comes to a close, a sense of psychological stability returns. There is a return home: Odysseus finds rest with his devoted and more than sufficiently reliable wife, Penelope, and he reclaims possession of his kingdom. But journeying, and the road, and the companionship of Hermes do not become mere remembrances of things past, good stories by the fire. They are retained as present reality and future necessity. For Odysseus's mission, discovered in Hades, is yet to be fulfilled. The oar must still be planted.

So the road winds on. And with companionable Hermes, *Koinos* Hermes, life after midlife continues to be a journey with soul.

References

Athanassakis, A. N., trans. (1976). *The Homeric Hymns*. Baltimore and London: Johns Hopkins University Press.

Baudelaire, C. (1982). *Les Fleurs Du Mal*. Translated by Richard Howard. Boston: David R. Godine.

Brown, N. O. (1969). *Hermes the Thief*. New York: Vintage Books.

Buber, M. (1970). *I and Thou*. New York: Charles Scribner's Sons.

Dante, A. (1974). *The Divine Comedy: Hell*. Translated by Dorothy L. Sayers. Penguin Books.

Ellenberger, H. (1970). *The Discovery of the Unconscious*. New York: Basic Books.

Erdman, D. V., ed. (1982). *The Complete Poetry and Prose of William Blake*. Berkeley and Los Angeles: University of California Press.

Erikson, E. (1968). *Identity: Youth and Crisis*. New York: W. W. Norton.

Fellini, F. (1980). "Dream Report." *Dreamworks* 1/1: 5–6.

Funk and Wagnalls (1972). *Standard Dictionary of Folklore, Mythology, and Legend*. New York: Funk and Wagnalls.

Gennep, A. van (1960). *The Rites of Passage*. Translated by Monika B. Vizedom and Gabrielle L. Caffee. Chicago: University of Chicago Press.

Henderson, J. L. (1967). *Thresholds of Initiation*. Middletown: Wesleyan University Press.

Hillman, J. (1979). *The Dream and the Underworld*. New York: Harper & Row.

Homans, P. (1979). *Jung in Context*. Chicago: University of Chicago Press.

Jaffé, A. (1971). *From the Life and Work of C. G. Jung*. New York: Harper Colophon Books.

—— (1972). "The Creative Phases of Jung's Life." *Spring: An Annual of Archetypal Psychology and Jungian Thought* (1972) : 162–90.

Jung, C. G. (1953). *Psychology and Alchemy*. Collected Works, vol. 12. New York: Pantheon Books, 1953.

—— (1959a). *The Archetypes and the Collective Unconscious*. Collected Works, vol. 9, part 1. New York: Pantheon Books, 1959.

—— (1959b). *Aion: Researches into the Phenomenology of the Psyche*. Collected Works, vol 9, part 2. New York: Pantheon Books, 1959.

—— (1961). *Memories, Dreams, Reflections*. New York: Vintage Books.

—— (1963). *Psychology and Religion: West and East*. Collected Works, vol. 11. New York: Pantheon Books, 1963.

—— (1966). *Two Essays on Analytical Psychology*. Collected Works, vol. 7. New York: Pantheon Books, 1966.

—— (1967). *Alchemical Studies*. Collected Works, vol. 13. Princeton: Princeton University Press, 1967.

—— (1969). *The Structure and Dynamics of the Psyche*. Collected Works, vol. 8. Princeton University Press, 1969.

—— (1970a). *Symbols of Transformation*. Collected Works, vol. 5. Princeton: Princeton University Press, 1970.

—— (1970b). *Mysterium Coniunctionis*. Collected Works, vol. 14. Princeton: Princeton University Press, 1970.

—— (1976). *The Symbolic Life*. Collected Works, vol. 18. Princeton: Princeton University Press, 1976.

Kendall, L. (1980). "Suspect Saviors of Korean Hearths and Homes." *Asia*, May/June 1980, pp. 12–15, 46–47.

Kerényi, K. (1976). *Hermes, Guide of Souls*. Spring Publications.

—— (1979). *Goddesses of Sun and Moon*. Spring Publications.

Lattimore, R., trans. (1951). *The Iliad of Homer*. Chicago and London: University of Chicago Press.

—— (1967). *The Odyssey of Homer*. New York: Harper Colophon Books.

Levinson, D. (1978). *The Seasons of a Man's Life*. New York: Knopf.

Lopez-Pedraza, R. (1977). *Hermes and His Children*. Spring Publications.

Nicholi, A. M., ed. (1978). *The Harvard Guide to Modern Psychiatry*. Cambridge and London: Harvard University Press.

Nilsson, M. P. (1969). *Greek Piety*. New York: W. W. Norton.

Onians, R. B. (1973). *The Origins of European Thought*. New York: Arno Press.

Otto, W. F. (1979). *The Homeric Gods*. London: Thames and Hudson.

Rahner, H. (1971). *Greek Myths and Christian Mystery*. New York: Biblo and Tannen.

Stein, J. O. (1981). "A Study of Change during the Midlife Transition in Men and Women, with Special Attention to the Intrapsychic Dimension." Ph.D. dissertation, Northwestern University.

Turner, V. W. (1967). *The Forest of Symbols*. Ithaca and London: Cornell University Press.

—— (1969). *The Ritual Process*. Chicago: Aldine.

Also from Spring Publications

Athene: Virgin and Mother KARL KERÉNYI
The Awesome Goddess who affects the fates of both women and men. Athene unites the virginal father's-daughter and the encouraging mother of the spirit. Mythological background of communal and political consciousness, individuality, and the power of mind. With a psychological postscript by Murray Stein. Scholarly apparatus, index. (106 pp.)

Goddesses of Sun and Moon KARL KERÉNYI
Circe, the enchantress; Medea, the murderess; Aphrodite, the golden one; and Niobe of the Moon. Configurations of feminine existence by the major mythological scholar of modern times. Only English translation of these papers, by Murray Stein. (84 pp.)

Facing the Gods JAMES HILLMAN, ed.
Nine chapters show how major figures of the Greek mythological imagination still work in the modern psyche as archetypal backgrounds for personal experiences in relationships, symptoms, actions, and dream imagery. Includes: Murray Stein (*Hephaistos*), David Miller (*Rhea*), Karl Kerényi (*Artemis*), Chris Downing (*Ariadne*), James Hillman (*Athene* and *Dionysos*), etc. Index. (172 pp.)

The Book of Life MARSILIO FICINO
This underground classic of the Italian Renaissance was once suppressed for Ficino's approach to images, daemons, and planets in relation to health. In this fluent and exact translation by Charles Boer—the first into English—the book is a guide to food, drink, sleep, mood, sexuality, song, and countless herbal and vegetable concoctions for maintaining the right balance of soul, body, and spirit. Translator's introduction, with bibliography, index. (xx, 217 pp.)

Patterns of Creativity Mirrored in Creation Myths
MARIE-LOUISE VON FRANZ
How did the ancients and other cultures conceive of creativity? What has happened to it in the contemporary world? These and other urgent questions find answers in this remarkable commentary upon creation myths assembled according to their basic thematic motifs. Index. (250 pp.)

Archetypal Medicine ALFRED J. ZIEGLER
In a clear and elegantly simple style, packed with case histories and medical data, Dr. Ziegler offers psychological readings of asthma, skin disease, heart attacks, anorexia, rheumatism, and chronic pain. Challenges the philosophy which furnishes the basis of traditional medicine, exposes its shadow, and charges that the excessive interest in health betrays humanity's deepest nature which is neither natural nor healthy but instead afflicted and chronically ill. (169 pp.)

Spring Publications, Inc. P.O. Box 222069 Dallas, Texas 75222